THE
HISTORY AND TEACHINGS

OF THE

EARLY CHURCH

AS A BASIS FOR

THE

RE-UNION OF CHRISTENDOM

Lectures

DELIVERED UNDER THE AUSPICES OF THE CHURCH
CLUB, IN CHRIST CHURCH, N. Y.

WIPF & STOCK · Eugene, Oregon

Wipf and Stock Publishers
199 W 8th Ave, Suite 3
Eugene, OR 97401

The History and Teachings of the Early Church as a Basis for the Re-Union of Christendom: Lectures Delivered Under the Auspices of the Church Club, In Christ Church, N. Y.
By Coxe, A. Cleveland
Softcover ISBN-13: 978-1-6667-6238-9
Hardcover ISBN-13: 978-1-6667-6239-6
eBook ISBN-13: 978-1-6667-6240-2
Publication date 10/13/2022
Previously published by E. & J. B. Young & Co., 1889

This edition is a scanned facsimile of the original edition published in 1889.

PREFACE.

THE lectures published in this volume were delivered in Christ Church, in this city, during the spring of 1888, under the auspices of the Church Club, an association of laymen of this diocese who have banded themselves together with this object, among others, of promoting the spread of sound Church doctrine and building up a robust churchmanship among the people.

This course of lectures was the first effort of the Church Club in this direction.

The subject chosen, that which gives the general title to the whole course, namely, "*The History and Teachings of the Early Church as a Basis for the Reunion of Christendom*," is eminently suggestive, in view of the recent utterances of our American House of Bishops, and of the Bishops assembled at the Lambeth Conference, on the subject of reunion and unity, and the erroneous constructions that some have put upon their words.

We regard the Reunion of Christendom as impossible except upon the basis of the faith and discipline of the Early Church, and to ascertain what those are, men must study her history.

Two facts stand out in bold relief in Catholic Christianity, considered from the historic standpoint:

First. The historic ministry, tracing its descent back without break or interruption to the Apostles' times, and commonly and correctly described as the Ministry of the Apostolic Succession.

Second. The fact that all Bishops are equal as touching their office, and that our Lord committed the supreme government of His Church to the Apostles and their successors, that is to say, to the collective Episcopate, and not to any one individual Bishop.

These facts appear to be strongly brought out in these lectures, which on that account alone deserve attention; but when the names and ability of the prelates and theologians who delivered them are taken into account, the volume may be cordially recommended not only to members of our communion, but also to those thoughtful men not in communion with us who are earnestly pondering the great question of Christian Unity.

CONTENTS.

LECTURE I.

THE PENTECOSTAL AGE.................................. 1
    By the Rt. Rev. A. Cleveland Coxe, D.D.

LECTURE II.

SYRIAN CHRISTIANITY AND THE SCHOOL OF ANTIOCH..... 31
    By Rev. Thomas Richey, D.D.

LECTURE III.

THE NORTH AFRICAN CHURCH AND ITS TEACHERS........ 59
    By Rev. J. F. Garrison, D.D.

LECTURE IV.

THE SCHOOL OF ALEXANDRIA 111
    By Rev. John H. Egar, D.D.

LECTURE V.

THE CHURCH OF ROME IN HER RELATION TO CHRISTIAN UNITY 169
    By the Rt. Rev. George F. Seymour, S.T.D., LL.D.

The Pentecostal Age and Growth of the Church to the Death of Saint John.

LECTURE I.

THE RT. REVEREND A. CLEVELAND COXE, D.D.,
Bishop of Western New York.

THE PENTECOSTAL AGE.

OUR times are grievous to be borne. For, to Christians, no material prosperity, no brilliant discoveries of science in its dealings with the world of sense, in short nothing that is temporal, and hence transient, can afford any satisfaction in exchange for a firm foothold upon the rock of faith in the Son of God, an eye uplifted in hope of immortality, and a heart full of love to humanity in all its needs, chiefly those which pertain to things eternal. But, to these great and lasting concerns, our times are indifferent, coldly skeptical, or malevolently hostile. "The enemy comes in like a flood," but true to His promise, just at such a crisis, "the Spirit of the Lord uplifts a standard against him."

Before this enemy those who love the Lord Jesus Christ feel the need of presenting a united front. Hence, a spirit of return to first principles is characteristic of the epoch among believers. Never, in modern times, have faith and zeal been more active: never before have learning and genius been more conspicuously enlisted on the side of divine revelation; never before have more rapid movements been made for a witness to heathen nations, and for claiming the utmost parts of the earth for the kingdom of Messiah. At such a moment the Spirit of God moves over the chaos of divisions and scandals, and his generative and constructive forces are felt anew. The demand for unity is the most hopeful feature of the age, and He who has inspired it will, I cannot but hope, bring it to good effect.

But, here, we encounter a new class of perils. Men devise schemes and projects of union which have no reference to those imperishable and fundamental principles, by the sacrifice of which all our schisms and scandals have been created. In our American republic, the Church of which we are members has ever been recognized as singular, as alone bearing a testimony concerning those organic laws of unity, which our Christian brethren have commonly accused of narrowness and bigotry. Doubtless truth itself may be maintained in a spirit essentially schismatical, because unloving and inconsiderate. The orthodoxy of the Pharisee may be hateful to God; the piety of the Samaritan may be preferred before it. Yet our Lord did not suffer the Samaritan woman to imagine that truth is unimportant; he reminded her that "salvation is of the Jews." We must "speak the truth in love"—

live the truth in love, as the text implies; but never must we be so "liberal" as to give away what does not belong to us. We must never compromise truth, in our haste to exhibit an unreal and disappointing union which is not unity and which is built upon the sand. We cannot surrender the vital unity of the Catholic and Apostolic Church to any sentiment of mere hand-shaking fraternity, which ignores the creed and the sacraments, and all that is essential for the perpetuity of their faithful ministration to the souls of men.

Here then we are met by a not unnatural outcry, that we are proposing unity only on conditions of entire conformity with our own local Church. Quite the reverse is true. We plead for a Universal System, in which we are included, but we make no stand on anything peculiar to ourselves. We are simply proposing that all should conform to the Holy Catholic and Apostolic Church, in things scriptural and historically accepted from the beginning. This is not ours to enact, much less to compromise. It is Law for all Christians. We accept it as ruled for us by those whom Christ had empowered to do so; had sent the Holy Spirit to guide; had promised to sustain; "binding in heaven what they should bind on earth." We lay on others nothing because it is ours. They are left to the largest freedom of details; they may use rites and ceremonies and prayers unknown to us. They may maintain them in full profession of the one faith.

They will then far outnumber us, and may take the land in possession. We shall rejoice and exult therein. They will, then, officiate at our altars, even if not prepared to welcome us to theirs. They often seem to take pleasure in representing us as a small body dictating to our superiors in numbers. But numbers beyond numbering have spoken thus, alike to us and them. In all charity, let them reflect that they may amuse themselves with a fallacy, and lose sight of historic truth and of the logic of unalterable facts. What they imagine us to dictate, comes to us and them alike, by the testimony of the historic Church of Christ, and by her universal legislation in ages, while as yet unity was unbroken. That unity was violated by the Bishop of Rome in the ninth century. The old constitutions and canons were ignored by him, as they now are by all the sects which originated in the sixteenth century; victims of the intolerable yoke his schism had imposed on the West. His new canons and fabulous decretals had been substituted for Laws of the Primitive Christians, and this created all the schisms of Western Christendom. The ignorance of early Christianity which had overspread the Latin churches bred a fatal mistake. Luther and Calvin failed to restore, while they strove to reform. They forgot that true *reformation* means nothing destructive, but implies the preservation of that which requires reform. You do not break what you undertake to cleanse. A golden vase may be encrusted with filthy accumulations, and may have been gilded over its very dirt; but you reform it by purging the dross, and by purifying. The moment you destroy the gold because of its defilement, you cease to be a reformer; you become a destroyer, and not a repairer. Now, what says the law of God? "If thou *take forth the precious from the vile*, thou shalt be as my mouth." This is restoration, and it is the *only* true reformation that can be recognized in the case of the Church; for old it is and defiled it may be, but it cannot perish without a failure of Christ's promise, nor can any man found a new church in its stead. It is an organization, a visible kingdom which was established eighteen hundred years ago, and which may be as foul as Sardis without losing its identity. This the Master recognized in His message to the corrupt churches of antiquity; and therefore, though the Latin churches be as wicked as Jezebel, and hateful as the Nicolaitanes, Christ's message to them one and all is only this: "Remember from whence thou art fallen, repent and do the first works." In a word, restore what is primitive in faith, in works, in order, in unity.

The path to unity, then, is a very plain one. Take a body of Christians, for example, like the Lutherans; the historic "Protestants," so universally honoured for their history of intrepid and suffering fidelity to certain great central truths. Is it anything which they ought to dread, this idea that something remains for them to do now, which could not be done amid the wars and confusions and persecutions of the past? Let us imagine a "Lutheran of the Lutherans" rising up in Germany and saying—"We have lost ground, and Rome has come back like a flood, where once we had fought and conquered. Let us see what mistakes were made; and what remains to be done, if we would go on and reform our own glorious Germany. It is ignoble to fold our hands and consent to live on as a feeble sect, while Germany is unreformed, and while a fouler superstition than that of the Middle Ages holds millions of Latin Christians in spiritual bondage. Let us wake up the reformation and repair our mistakes; let us do what remains to be done, instructed by the history of three centuries; let us go on to do for Germany what Luther wished to do; what John Huss and Jerome of Prague might have done more successfully perhaps; what we may do by falling back upon their lines and carrying on what they so gloriously begun." Let us imagine, I say, such a Lutheran raised up, by God's mighty power, to complete the reformation, by the work that remains to be done—that is, the work of RESTORATION? Is there anything in all this that any Lutheran should not rejoice to do? Very well; to come back to our own land: Suppose some Lutheran here should say— these "Episcopalians" are Laodiceans; they utterly fail to do the work God has set before them; they do not recognize what even De Maistre saw to be their special mission. Let us not wait for them ; let us learn from De Maistre what is really " precious " in their possessions ; but, since they have laid it up in a napkin, let us take the lead and do for them and for ourselves together, what ought to be done. Let us begin the work of Universal Restoration. Let us go to our countrymen, the Old Catholics of Germany ; let us obtain the historic organization which is useful, to say the least, and on which hinges so much that is essential to peace. Thus qualified, let us appeal to other Christians to unite with us. We shall, in time, enfold the great mass of American piety and zeal and learning in a truly Apostolic American Church ; a church tolerant of local differences, but confessing the Apostolic Faith and maintaining an organic Unity ; all "striving together " for " the faith once delivered to the saints." Let some Lutheran, I say, be raised up here, in America, to meet the gigantic problems of the land in such a spirit—what would become of us " Episcopalians ? " Why, the answer is—we should be swallowed up, absorbed, and unified in this great body, and we should sing *Alleluias* over such a consummation. Perish every thought of ambition or of narrow devotion to our own local history, that should stand in the way of a consummation so glorious. Let our fellow-Christians rise up to a work so blessed, and they may be sure that they will encounter no opposition from us. We should be found working with them and for them. In functional details we should daily no doubt draw nearer and nearer together, and so organic Unity might be restored in God's good time. We do not say "come over to us," therefore we do not propose to go over to you. But, when we all consent to the Universal Law of System, and gravitate to the Common Centre of Catholic and Primitive and Scriptural Truth—then the work is done. There we all meet, and there we all become One in Christ and His Church. Thus, too, we shall defeat what is Roman in the alien immigration, by embracing all that is Catholic in it. Thus Romanists will have come to America to be reformed; they will become "Old Catholics" first; and then, one with their fellow-Christians, in the great American Church of the future.

I have put the case in a form of imaginary progress, sufficiently humiliating to ourselves. It is hard even to think of ourselves as so utterly unworthy to help others. But, such is our answer to a stale complaint of arrogance on our part of which it effectually disposes.

I might easily point out the elements which exist among American sects, for this great restoration; to be wrought out by themselves, and so made real and lasting; but this is not my duty now. As introductory to the course which has been so admirably outlined, I have ventured upon a train of thought which, I trust, will guard against mistakes within or without our own fold. Let me now congratulate you on your noble efforts to become rooted and grounded in the fundamental principles of Unity, which it is our mission to uphold, leaving results to God ; so reaching just conclusions as to what is to be conceded under the law of liberty, and what is to be defended and maintained as truth belonging to God, which no weak yearning for sentimental good has any excuse for compromising. I am very glad that it falls to me to go over the scriptural ground of the first century. I hold, indeed, that the second century is evidence of what the apostles delivered to the Church of the primitive age; for he who thinks otherwise must confront the absurd conclusion that the whole church committed suicide as soon as the apostles fell asleep, by rejecting divine ordinances and constitutions and modes of worship, and " the faith once delivered to the saints." It is the simple statement of the Anglican Church, that certain things are " evident to all men diligently reading the Holy Scripture and ancient authors." The ancient authors must keep their place ; they are merely witnesses, and help us to determine whether anything we seem to see in the Scriptures are only our private whim. If what we read in the New Testament is found to coincide with what we find in the writings of Clement and Ignatius and Polycarp, then, by all rules of evidence, we are assured of our position. It is a maxim which rules in all courts of law, that " the contemporary interpretation of any law or ordinance is the strongest and must prevail."

We come, then, to the Pentecostal period. The Holy Ghost was not only to guide the apostles into all truth; He was to "bring to their remembrance" all things which Christ Himself had told them. It will be recalled that after our Lord had risen from the dead, the apostles themselves were yet full of Jewish ideas, and were only gradually awakened to the universal inclusiveness of their commission and of their appointed work. The story of St. Peter's vision at Joppa, and of the baptism of Cornelius, proves this. The Holy Ghost was that "other Comforter" who was to open their hearts and minds to the whole of what their Master had designed. During the great forty days, He had been seen of them after His resurrection, and He had then taught them "the things pertaining to *the kingdom* of God." Now, in the Acts and the Apostolic Epistles we have the record of these same things. What the apostles ruled and wrought and wrote are the things "pertaining to the kingdom," which the Master ordained, and which the Holy Ghost brought to their remembrance. Entire unity of system runs through and regulates all, in all the Epistles. If we find any one rule laid down by any apostle, that is what all the apostles "ordained in all the churches." To all alike were given "the keys of the kingdom;" all "spake by the same Spirit." To the whole College of the Apostles was given the promise that "what they bound on earth should be bound in heaven." The "Unity of the Spirit;" the Communion of

Saints in that one Spirit; the "one Lord, one Faith, one Baptism;" these are the outgrowth of that period, which is delineated for us in the Book of the Acts, the " Gospel of the Holy Ghost."

So, then, let us come to one of those imperial texts, which flood with light all that is elsewhere recorded concerning the primitive faithful. Here it is, in the history of the great day of Pentecost itself, when the Catholic Church received the first outpouring of the Holy Ghost. " Then they that gladly received his word, were (1) baptized, and the same day there were added to them about three thousand souls. And they continued steadfastly in (2) the apostles' doctrine, and (3) fellowship, and (4) in the breaking of bread, and (5) the prayers." Here are all the elements of Catholic Unity. St. Peter's great privilege of being the first to confess the Incarnate God had been rewarded by the privilege of a primacy peculiar to himself, and in its own nature incommunicable to others.[1] His was the first use of the keys, in opening the kingdom to Jews and then to Gentiles. But, there St. Peter's distinction ends. The same keys and the same authority were given to all the apostles in corporate unity. Hence St. Peter *received* mission from the Apostolic College, instead of giving it. The apostles "*sent* Peter and John" into Samaria to confirm those whom St. Philip had baptized. In the first council it is St. James who presides, and not St. Peter. St. Paul disputes with

[1] Acts xv. 7.

St. Peter, and the Holy Ghost ratifies what St. Paul had maintained against him. St. Paul is permitted by the Spirit to record that he received nothing from James, Peter, or John, "who seemed to be pillars," and that he was "not a whit behind the very chiefest of the apostles." Christ himself had settled beforehand, that no one among them was to "be greatest." He hinted to them that there were "last who should be first," and this was fulfilled in the subsequent primacy of St. James, and in the universal mission of St. Paul to the Gentiles, while St. Peter's jurisdiction was expressly restricted to the Jewish dispersion. St. Cyprian thinks that our Lord's twofold act was significant: first, he gave the keys as signifying one indivisible power; then he gave the same to all the apostles to signify that all had the same right to use it. Here, then, we have the nature of "the apostles' fellowship" defined. It is not communion with St. Peter, nor with any one Apostolic See; it is the communion and fellowship of the apostles maintained, (1) by their baptism, (2) their doctrine, and (3) by "continuing steadfastly" therein, as opposed to becoming followers of any one teacher, or joining any sect originating subsequently to the foundation of the Christian Church, thus organized once for all and forever, under the guidance of the Holy Spirit.

The apostolic eucharist and the apostolic prayers, here referred to, show that a system of worship was recognized by the Church from the beginning, as that in which all Christians were to continue steadfastly. This was none other than the synagogue worship augmented by Christian "hymns and spiritual songs," which lifted the Psalter into the Christian substance that had been so long veiled under the Law, and which Christ, in the walk to Emmaus, had expounded in its fulness of relation to Himself. Such were the apostolic prayers, while the apostolic "breaking of bread" succeeded the bloody sacrifices of the Law, and fulfilled the prediction of Malachi concerning "the pure oblation" in every place among the Gentiles. This St. Paul refers to. He asserts it to be part of his great commission to secure this to the Gentiles as their "liturgist and hierurge;" for so the Greek records it.

We now come to the enlargement of the Apostolic College by the commission of "Barnabas and Paul;" and subsequently by the admission of others, who are distinguished from the apostles of Christ's personal ordaining, as "apostles (or angels) of *the churches*." Here was signified (1) Christ's intention to perpetuate the apostolic order, and (2) the co-equal power of the Holy Ghost to do this for Christ. Then (3) we come to the formation of what is now called the "Apostolic Episcopate," *i.e.*, the succession of those chosen to the presidency of the churches by the churches themselves. These received the ordinary gifts (but not the *extraordinary* functions) of the original apostles of Christ.

Our Lord intended the Apostolic order to be perpetual in His Church: " He was to be with *them* always, to the end of the world." Not with them personally, of course, but with the Apostolic Ministry. The other orders were founded by the Apostles themselves. They were " also presbyters;" and they appointed *co-presbyters*, as well as co-apostles; they were " deacons," and they appointed an order of deacons to relieve them of their inferior ministries. But, to Timothy and Titus personally, as co-apostles, they gave co-apostolic power to *ordain* presbyters and deacons. No such powers were lodged with the presbytery, though they assisted in laying on hands when persons were admitted to their order. Thus, Titus was stationed in Crete to " ordain presbyters in every city." He was the ordainer; otherwise it would have been sufficient to leave a presbytery to " ordain in every city," when once two or three presbyters had been ordained to start with.

Here let me note, once for all, that not names, but things, are thus spoken of. The original *names* of these officers were (1) " Apostles of Christ," or " Apostles of the Churches;" (2) presbyters, or elders, and (3) deacons. They were sometimes spoken of less technically, and hence confused ideas have arisen. Apostles and presbyters were *bishops, i.e.*, pastors, and we still speak of both orders alike as pastors. The presbyters of Crete were pastors of their flocks in certain cities; but Titus was pastor " *in every city* " of Crete, and had the presbyters also in his jurisdiction, as appears from the Epistle. More strikingly this principle appears in the two Epistles to Timothy: He presides over the local presbyters, who were pastors (or "bishops") in Ephesus; but he, while not less a co-presbyter, is alone empowered to ordain. He himself had been ordained a presbyter "*by* St. Paul, *with* the presbytery," and he is reminded not to neglect his presbyter-work because he had also a superior place and task. It is noteworthy that the term "presbyters," like *pastors* now, was a term often used in speaking of the two higher orders, long after the term "bishops" had become peculiar to one of them. Those who had succeeded to apostolic powers delighted to imitate St. Peter and speak of themselves a *co-presbyters ;* and of their brethren presbyters as *co-bishops*, that is, overseers or pastors of their several flocks. The fallacy of arguing, therefore, that these were overseers *in the same degree* is most apparent. Little by little the modest term of bishops (to which presbyters had a right in a lower degree) became restricted to pastors-in-chief; who thus resigned forever, to those chief apostles of Scripture, and especially to those who were filled with the *extraordinary* gifts needful in founding the Church, that venerable name. Again, I remark, we have been speaking of *things*, not mere *names*. These things are the three orders, distinctly marked as in other scriptures, so also more emphatically and definitely in the Epistles to Timothy and Titus. Epaphroditus was the "apostle" of the Philippians, and carried to his presbyters and deacons the epistle which St. Paul wrote to them, to account for his long absence and to fortify them in their love to their Diocesan; so that this epistle is hardly less explicit. And here let it be said, once for all, that if any other theory of the Primitive Ministry be adopted, it is impossible to interpret the Acts and Epistles in a symmetrical and harmonious way, meeting all cases and all points without straining anything. On the other hand, this system involves no other difficulty than a confusion of *words* or *names*, out of which the schoolmen framed the Presbyterial theory, in order to lower the bishops to the order of presbyters, and thus to exalt the Pope as the one and only Bishop properly so called. It seems strange, but it is not less true, that in this our denominational brethren are the victims of the Papacy. In fact they are the only Christians who accept the Papal dogma by which *Presbyters* are made the highest order in the Christian Ministry. Romish bishops by their laws are only presbyters, admitted to Episcopal *functions*, as vicars of the Universal Bishop, or Pope. Their dogma affirms that the holy orders are three, " presbyters, deacons, and *sub-deacons*," and that these three orders have existed since the apostles' times! This is palpably a falsehood as regards *sub-deacons;* and it is needless to say that the Greek churches, with all the Fathers, recognize the threefold ministry as "bishops, presbyters, and deacons;" that is in scriptural terms "apostles, elders, and deacons;" phraseology, which I have sufficiently explained.

The formation of the Historic Episcopate is thus expounded; but I have anticipated in some degree as to the process. All becomes more absolutely and unanswerably evident, if we return to the enlargement of the Episcopate, or rather of the Apostolate, by the admission of others to the company of the eleven. The case of Matthias is exceptional. St. Peter's language about his election, his reference to the minatory psalm, and his exposition of its force, like his great sermon on the day of Pentecost, are full of ideas wholly unlike anything that precedes the "Walk to Emmaus" and the "Great Forty Days." All this reflects the Master's own teachings concerning His kingdom after His resurrection. Exceptionally, and to fulfil the Scriptures, therefore, Matthias in place of Judas becomes an apostle under the command—" his *bishopric* let another take." But this was only his call; his qualification was that of the Holy Ghost, given to him as to the eleven, on the day of Pentecost, when the fiery tongues completed the investiture of the Apostolic College. It was thus rendered what it had been before, an unmutilated company of original eye-witnesses of the Incarnate Word.

Two more were, soon after, added to this company, in exceptional ways; and this enlargement of the Apostolic College disposes of all theories based on any idea that the number of the apostles was in fact limited to twelve. This idea receives, it is true, a momentary colour when, in the Apocalypse, the "twelve foundations" are spoken of, and the "twelve apostles of the Lamb." Just so "the twelve sons of Jacob" are spoken of, though in the Apocalypse Dan is omitted and Ephraim is not mentioned, except under the name of Joseph; while like Manasseh, his brother, he is only Jacob's grandson, not literally his son. It is not easy to harmonize this catalogue with that of Jacob on his deathbed. So we read of "the four-and-twenty elders." Who are they? Secret things belong to God, and nobody is called to harmonize them before His time. Obviously they do not affect the recorded facts that Barnabas and Saul were added to the original College of the Apostles.

On one point St. Paul always insists: he is an apostle "of our Lord Jesus Christ." He does so, because there were apostles "of the churches." Our Lord had personally called him; he was "not of men," like false apostles, "nor by men," like the "apostles of the churches." These latter were *successors* of the apostles; but he and Barnabas, in divers ways, were called to be of the original college. The original apostles recognized [1] them as such, giving them "the right hand of fellowship;" but it is instructive to note an underlying principle here, which amounts to this, viz., that an apostle called by Christ

[1] Galat. ii. 9.

himself, and an apostle called by Christ through His Holy Spirit, are of like character, and as such co-equals. Barnabas is said to have had a call from the Spirit previous to that recorded of his mission; St. Paul had been called and made an apostle previously. Both received their *mission*, not their *order*, from the Holy Ghost through inspired prophets. The original apostles recognized them as *aggregated* to their own company, not as successors, but as apostles, by original and underived commission; "*perceiving*," says St. Paul, "the grace that was given unto *me*," that I, as well as Barnabas, "should go unto the Gentiles." Those who fail to distinguish between order and mission find difficulties in this history, most of which disappear if this distinction is made. But even the Independents, I am informed, practically recognize the difference; that is, they regard, a certain brother as a qualified preacher of the gospel, but when he is elected to be the pastor of a particular flock, they unite in "settling him," which they do with a form called "the right hand of fellowship." In other words, they give him *mission* after their manner. Apply the like idea to the inspired mission of two apostles; the one of whom received his apostleship *directly* from Christ personally, while the other received the same *indirectly* from Christ, through His divine Spirit. Then, they received *mission*, from the Holy Spirit, through inspired men commanded to solemnize the gift. Their entire equality with the original college of apostles demonstrates the power of the Holy Ghost to ordain and qualify ministers of Christ through all time, and till the second coming of our Lord.

The secondary class of apostles is called that of "apostles of the churches" by St. Paul. The Greek word (*angelos*), or "*angel* of the churches," is equipollent—a mere synonym—and is used by St. John as he uses a word for "the Lamb," different from what is used elsewhere, but entirely equivalent. His mind, in both cases, probably reverted to the original Syriac, as when he uses "Cephas" instead of Peter, in the story of that apostle.

The passage in which St. Paul uses this distinction is very striking, and is a key to other passages. Thus he says, in his second Epistle to the Corinthians:[1] "Whether any do inquire of Titus, he is my partner and fellow-helper concerning you; or our brethren be inquired of, they are *the apostles of the churches* and the glory of Christ." Thus he defines the apostleship of those whom he employed as "fellow-helpers," and about whose *status* the Corinthians were apparently puzzled. When Christ appears to St. John, "holding seven stars in his right hand"—these stars receive the same name—"angels (or apostles) of the seven churches," and their starry similitude indicates this "glory of Christ;" dimmed and clouded as was the lustre of some of these seven, who were yet recognized by the long-suffering author of their ministry. If then such

[1] II. Cor. viii. 27.

be "inquired after," in the case of Apollos, or Silas, or Sosthenes, or Timothy, or Titus, or others, here is the answer: Though not primary apostles, they were yet Christ's apostles, as being chosen by, or divinely set over, certain churches, or appointed to be coadjutors of other apostles, as were Linus and Cletus at Rome. When we come to a later period, we find Timothy and Titus *localized* in Ephesus and Crete; and later still, we find seven churches of Asia, with their localized "angels." Thus, the diocesan Episcopate was formed before the death of St. John, and accepted by our Lord himself, as appears in what "the Spirit saith unto the churches."

Whatever interpretation may be put upon Scripture, however, by methods which depend upon the ambiguities of certain words, we reach historic facts of the second century which point to one conclusion only in the records of the Church. Here we find not a trace of any other system than that which I have delineated. Call him what you will, for in his humility, amid the simplicity and suffering estate of all Christians about him, he assumed no titles of pre-eminence and was "also a presbyter;" call him, therefore, what you may, one always presides over the presbytery and administers the affairs of any local church under the instructions given to Timothy and Titus. He ordains presbyters; the presbytery assists in the ordination, but *never ordains without him.* He alone administers discipline, receives and tries accusations, exhorts and rebukes with authority, and guides the flock as the common father of the people and their pastor as well. The Epistles of Clement and of Polycarp only incidentally illustrate this condition of things, but their contemporary Ignatius makes them the subject of his letters to the churches of Asia and to Polycarp, his beloved brother, as he goes to Rome to die a martyr. In that crisis he felt the importance of entire unity among the churches, and of that holy spirit of order and brotherly love in local churches which alone could prevent schisms and heresies from cropping out and devouring the flock, as St. Paul had foretold. We may fearlessly challenge the Papacy to produce anything, in this primitive period, to support its presbyterial theory; which makes bishops in no respect other than presbyters, empowered by one universal bishop at Rome to represent *his* authority, by *his* permission only; not acting as empowered by Christ, in perfect equality with all the bishops of Christendom, whether at Rome or Antioch. We may just as confidently challenge Presbyterians to show, anywhere in the history of ages preceding the time of Calvin, any token of a church constituted on Calvin's theory. But his theory was an honest mistake, derived from his scholastic education. He had been always led to suppose that bishops were, what Rome makes them, mere presbyters deriving their episcopal functions from the pope. He accepted the scholastic doctrine that presbyters are the highest order in the ministry. What follows in his mind is strictly logical. He argues thus: If then the Papacy is a fiction (as is evident enough), bishops, who are only the pope's vicars, must disappear also, for shadows cannot exist without a substance. Thus he argued and created Presbyterianism; most reasonably, if we grant the purely Papal premises on which he reasoned. And yet, even Calvin, who had never seen many of the early Christian writers now in our hands, recognizes the existence in primitive ages of a pure Episcopacy, derived from Christ and not from the Pope, in which one presbyter presides over the brotherhood; and he declares that "there is no anathema" which would not be deserved by anyone unwilling to accept such an Episcopacy. To the honour of English Presbyterians in the seventeenth century, they, therefore, placed their fundamental principle not on the exclusion of bishops, but on the admission of presbyters and laymen to a share in the synodical regimen of churches; and they professed themselves ready, with this concession, to return to the Church of England. The concessions which they demanded as to presbyters and laity, in synods, are made in our American Church.

Here then is the interpretation of ages; of primitive antiquity and of universal consent; as to the meaning of Scripture and the ordinances of the Apostles empowered by the Holy Ghost. East and West, alike, all the Councils and all the Fathers of the first ages are agreed as to this. Nor does even the paradoxical and vindictive Jerome, magnifying his order as a presbyter against the ambitious deacons of his day, say anything practically different; though his rhetorical extravagances undoubtedly laid the egg which the schoolmen hatched when they pulled down bishops to magnify a pope. The Greek churches, to this day, and all the Easterns, who have never recognized the papacy, exhibit the unchanged system of the early Church, as an irrefragable evidence of what I have thus presented.

So, then, he who rejects this system must not only confront these historic facts, but he must face another dilemma, not less confounding. If the Presbyterian or other similar theory was that of the Apostolic ordinances, how comes it that before St. John had ceased to teach and to preside in the infant Church, all traces of this theory had so utterly disappeared? How comes it that nobody protested against the changes introduced? That no presbytery resisted the elevation of one of their brethren to a permanent presidency over them? That no historian tells us anything of this utter transformation of Church Order? That not a single church existed or was heard of, at the time of the first Christian Council, that was not constructed in the Episcopal polity? That nobody ever hinted or imagined, in those days, that there had been a world-wide revolution of ideas and of organization in the Christian Church, since the apostles fell asleep? Well does Chillingworth argue that the metamorphoses of Mythology or of Arabian fables would be credible, if anybody could credit that the Apostolic churches were Presbyterian, but somehow, in a single night as it were, were all turned into "Episcopalianism;" no man forbidding. And nobody has ever pretended to fix the date or give any evidence of a revolution the most marvellously radical and universal that can be imagined.

Hence, after the study of the Pentecostal age in Holy Scripture, we come to ancient authors as a school-boy comes to the "proof" of his simple arithmetical processes. If the entire Church is found, at the close of this period, united in a system of doctrine and polity such as we have derived from Holy Scripture, the concurrence *proves* our conclusions to be true. By the destruction of this ancient polity all our divisions have been created; we ask a return then to this historic system, as the only solution of our difficulties. This the Catholic (Nicene) Church requires, hence, on this point, we can make no compromise. It is not ours to give; to yield is not liberality, but treason to Truth. To insist in a spirit of love is the highest charity to our brethren, who cannot be restored to Catholic unity on any other base. The conclusion of the whole matter then is this, Calvin himself bearing witness: Since God has restored, in many places, that early system which was the safeguard of unity and in which were digested all the Scriptural and Primitive Constitutions of Unity; and in which an Episcopate exists dependent upon Christ and not upon a Papacy; and in which presbyters and laymen may have their share in Synodical Legislation; it is the duty of all Christians to heal our divisions by returning to this system. Returning to this *system*, I say; I do not ask them to join us; but, when they organize themselves, accordingly, they will let us join them, I trust. I dare not use Calvin's strong language; he *anathematizes* all who would reject this system, should it be attainable. It would be contrary to my views of duty to anathematize anybody; but what I say is this: It is time for our Presbyterian brethren to study the laws of unity, and to do so in the spirit of that love to Christ, which, for His sake, would remove mountains. If so, they may restore to his family that *oneness*, which Christ Himself teaches us is the condition of the world's conversion. Hear His words: "That they all may be one. . . . That the world may believe that Thou hast sent Me." And this unity is made indivisible, like that of the Father and the Son, in the same passage of Holy Writ.

Observe the absolute unity of Christian organization as left by St. John. Return to these divine principles is the only possible base of the restoration. "Reformation" must be incomplete till thus crowned with positive conformity to the pattern in the Mount, for which a negative "protest" has been too long substituted. And let our brethren observe that in all this, as I have said, we propose nothing that is our own specialty. Not our prayer-book; not our Anglican ideas, prejudices, or customs; not our Anglo-American peculiarities; not in any sense unity *with us*—save as, by coming to unity with the historic Church of Christ, everywhere and as always prescribed, they compel us to meet them as Catholic and Apostolic brethren. Let them take their own courses; work out their own restoration in their own way, and all is done. We care not a straw for any triumph of our cause, or of our local church. We plead for the whole Church. Let them absorb us, and not the reverse, which they imagine is our ambition. Perish the thought! We dare not so think of it; we cherish " unfeigned love of the brethren," and in all we propose, it is the love of Christ that " constraineth us." For there is an example, in Holy Scripture, which in many ways meets their case. There was one learned, eloquent, and " mighty in the Scripture," who preached Christ with marvellous power and success. He was pre-eminently a preacher of the Gospel; he had no equal. What more can be said? Only this. He knew the Word of God; few knew it so well; but he had yet to learn that there is a "Way of God," clearly recognized as the institution of Christ and of His Holy Spirit, through inspired apostles. This glorious character, then, added humility the most profound to all his other qualities, and consented to learn the "Way of God" *more perfectly* from two of the humblest members of the Apostolic Church. Is it too much to ask of some noble Apollos that he would consent to learn, from all historic Christendom, " the Way of God *more perfectly?* " On this appeal, I rest my argument; and if it be not of God, may He raise up somebody to teach me His way, " more perfectly." May He give me the spirit never to harden my heart against godly men, who would speak to me their views of " Truth, in Love."

Syrian Christianity and the School of Antioch.

LECTURE II.

REV. THOMAS RICHEY, D.D.,

Professor of Ecclesiastical History in the General Theological Seminary, New York.

SYRIAN CHRISTIANITY AND THE SCHOOL OF ANTIOCH.

THE subject proposed for consideration to-night by the Church Club, is Syrian Christianity and the School of Antioch. It will not have escaped your observation—possibly it may have been the occasion of not a little surprise—that in the arrangement of these lectures a marked prominence has been given to a portion of the Church of Christ which has passed into almost total oblivion, having long since ceased to take any active part in the world's affairs. The arrangement has not been accidental. It was thought desirable, in connection with the cumulative character of the argument which it is the aim of these lectures to present, to give marked prominence at the outset to the fact that, long before Greek Christianity had begun its course in the East—before Roman Christianity had undertaken to play the part which it afterward did in the West—there was in existence a Church of which the Syrian Antioch was the centre and seat. In territorial extent the Syrian Church extended from the Mediterranean Sea in the West to the Caucasian Mountains and the Caspian Sea in the East; to the Erythrean Sea and the Persian Gulf on the South. It will be remembered, moreover, that Syrian Christianity was in an especial degree the creation of the great teacher of the Gentiles, S. Paul. It was at Antioch, in Syria, that S. Paul first entered upon the active duties of his ministry. Antioch was the centre of the first great missionary movement which had for its result the conversion of the Western world. The witness which a Church so widespread in its extent, and so mighty in its influence—Oriental, not Greek or Roman, in its character—bears to the primitive type of Christianity is of a peculiar kind. It is the witness of a Church which cannot be charged with excessive hierarchical pretension on the one hand, or with love of worldly power on the other. It brings us back to the Apostolic age, and the days when the Church, as the virgin bride of Christ, had not as yet entered into any entangling alliances with the powers of the world. Before Constantinople was founded—while Rome was still a pagan city—Antioch, for some three hundred years, was the centre of Christian influence for both East and West.

There is another reason why the Church of Syria is to be recognized as of special value in any study of the constitution and practice of the early Christian Church. It would seem to have been the purpose of Divine Providence to make special provision that the shoot, which in due course of time was to be transplanted from the Holy Land to grow and flourish in a foreign soil, should have prepared for its reception something of the nature of a forcing process, or hot-bed, where the plant will soon arrive at maturity, and opportunity shall also be given for everything of the nature of heretical pravity to develop itself speedily. It is a marked peculiarity of the Syrian Church in the East (as we shall find it to be also of the North African Church in the West,) that its disciples were men of warm and ardent temperament, who received Christianity with all the ardor and intensity of their nature, and were not satisfied to rest content with a religion of abstract propositions or mere logical conceptions. Christianity in Syria sprung in a moment, as it were, into a thriving and vigorous life. Churches grew and multiplied with a rapidity of which we know nothing in modern times. If they declined as rapidly as they came to life, it does not make the study of their growth and development less valuable, but more so.

When Jerusalem fell, Antioch became to the Christian world the centre of light and influence. It was at that time the third great city in the world. In some respects indeed it had no equal. Antioch could boast of three things which made it the pride and glory of ancient civilization. It had a situation unequalled, even by Constantinople itself. It lay under the shadow of the Lebanon, only sixteen miles distant from the Mediterranean. It was watered by the cool stream of the Orontes. Libanius tells us that every house in Antioch had an abundant supply of water, and enjoyed the luxury of the bath. The main street of the city was four and a half miles in length, and was paved with magnificent stones, so that it surpassed the great Roman highways. A corridor ran throughout the whole length of the street, by which the inhabitants were at once guarded from the heat of the sun in summer, and from exposure to rain and snow in winter. Libanius tells us moreover that the whole of that magnificent thoroughfare was lighted with lamps, so that the night could scarcely be distinguished from the day; he adds that Antioch was the only city of the ancient world which was so lighted. It was to this city—the great summer resort of the nations of the earth—in luxury of living the Paris of the time—that the Christians fled for refuge when, upon the martyrdom of Stephen, they were compelled to abandon Jerusalem and had to seek a new centre for the extension of the Christian faith. It was here that S. Paul began his missionary work, and went forth to the conversion of the nations.

The story is told of Alexander of Macedon, that he sat down to weep when he had no more worlds to conquer; we all know what it is which makes the name of Cæsar a name that is still remembered among men; but what was the work of Alexander of Macedon, or the conquests of Julius Cæsar, in comparison with the work which S. Paul, the great apostle and missionary of the Gentiles, set before him when he went forth from Antioch to plant the cross of Christ in every land? Never until that hour had it entered into the heart of man to conceive of uniting all men in the bonds of a common brotherhood, by proclaiming God to be the Father of us all. When the Jew looked out upon the world and thought of its conversion, he thought only of national conquest. But when S. Paul apprehended in all its fulness the mystery of the cross of Christ, all thoughts of national barriers and distinctions of race were obliterated and passed away forever. Antioch, for the first time in the history of mankind, became a missionary centre for the extension of the Gospel throughout the world. It was, as we have already seen, a city specially fitted for becoming the basis of operation for such a work. In situation it belonged to the Orient; by conquest it had become Greek; in course of time it passed from the Greeks into the hands of the Roman power. Antioch was in the broadest sense of the word a cosmopolitan city. Every country, every nationality had representatives there; it was a place eminently fitted to become the seat of a Catholic religion—a centre of light and influence for the whole world.

I count myself happy that, in the arrangement of these lectures, I have had assigned to me for a subject a topic of such very varied and surpassing interest as the Syrian Church and the see of Antioch. It would be difficult to find in all literature a more romantic story than that which is furnished by the history and fortunes of the Epistles of S. Ignatius, the second Bishop of the see of Antioch after the times of S. Peter and S. Paul. It was just after the discovery of the art of printing—about the year 1497—that there came to light in the West twelve epistles on which was inscribed the name of Ignatius. In addition to these, five others were found which bore the same name, but which upon comparison proved to be spurious compilations of a later age. Some time after, Archbishop Usher, in the course of his investigations in England—I think about the year 1644—discovered a Latin translation of the Seven Short Epistles (as they are called) of the great Syrian Father. Two years subsequently to this, there were discovered six Greek epistles by Vossius, which corresponded exactly with the Latin epistles of Archbishop Usher; and the year following, there was found in Florence an epistle of S. Ignatius to the Romans, which made the number of the seven short Greek epistles complete. Here, then, you have in existence twelve longer epistles in Latin claiming the name of Ignatius, with five admitted on all sides to be spurious; and seven shorter epistles, both in Greek and Latin, bearing the

SCHOOL OF ANTIOCH. 39

same honored name. The controversy on the whole subject of the Ignatian literature became at this time embittered by the introduction of a new element of religious strife. Upon the one side were arrayed those of the Continental Reformers who were opposed to Episcopacy, and who were disposed with Calvin to denounce the whole thing as a figment of a later age; on the other hand the great Pearson, in England, undertook the defence of the seven shorter epistles of Vossius and of Archbishop Usher. And now comes the third part of the story. In addition to the twelve Latin epistles and the seven shorter epistles in Latin and in Greek, Archdeacon Tatham, when travelling in the Holy Land in the year 1843, discovered in a monastery three epistles of S. Ignatius written in Syriac, and of a still shorter form than the Greek and Latin epistles of Vossius and Usher. You have in existence, then (in addition to the twelve original Latin epistles and the seven shorter epistles in Latin and in Greek), three Syriac epistles, differing from both in number and in form.

The controversy in England now assumed a new shape; the best scholars there (with the exception of the late Bishop of Lincoln) were disposed to accept the three short Syriac epistles as the genuine remains of S. Ignatius. But, just as the minds of English scholars were settling down in this conviction, Professor Peterman discovered an Armenian copy of the writings of Ignatius. This Armenian copy had the seven shorter Epistles of Vossius and Archbishop Usher.

The controversy entered again upon a new stage. The Bishop of Durham, the learned Dr. Lightfoot, had been disposed to accept the Syriac Epistles as the only genuine remains of S. Ignatius. But upon further consideration, after the discovery of Professor Peterman, he was induced to undertake a new examination of the whole question of the Ignatian literature. For thirty years he prosecuted his task. He had search made in every part of the known world, wherever any trace of the writings of Ignatius could be found; he examined, either in person or by deputy, every manuscript that was accessible in every library in Europe. The result has been the editing of the writings of the great Syriac Father, according to the best manuscripts, wherever found: and the declaration, after thirty years' of patient toil, upon authority that will not be questioned by any scholar of the nineteenth century, that the seven shorter Epistles of Vossius and of Archbishop Usher, as found in Latin and in Greek, are the true writings of S. Ignatius.

I know of nothing, in the history of either sacred or profane literature, more interesting than this. For not less than four hundred years has the controversy over the genuine writings of S. Ignatius been going on. It is a controversy which has enlisted in it some of the greatest names of modern times, and must now be regarded as set at rest forever.

But it is not the literature of the Ignatian Epistles that chiefly interests us to-night. The contest regarding the validity of the writings of S. Ignatius has been so protracted (and at times so intensely bitter), for the reason that on the testimony of S. Ignatius, more than any other of the early Fathers, depends the settlement of the vexed question of the Apostolic origin of the Episcopate, in opposition to the Calvinistic theory of Presbyterian Ordination. It is our own good fortune that in our day and generation that question has been finally settled. We are able to produce as a witness one who was the familiar and friend of a well-known disciple of S. John—the last link between the Apostolic and the post-Apostolic age. The witness is one, you will permit me again to remind you, who belongs neither to the later Greek Church of the East, nor to the Roman Church, but represents the earlier and virgin age of the Church, when the light kindled by S. John in Asia Minor still burned with an intense and ardent flame. What then is the testimony which S. Ignatius gives regarding the Church's unity, and as to the means of preserving it unbroken for the generations yet to come? In every one of his Epistles Ignatius asserts, with reiterated emphasis, that the Episcopate is the great bond of moral unity; that apart from the bishop, there is no approach to the altar; no way of entering into fellowship with the Church of the living God. To judge aright of the value of his testimony, you must call to mind the way in which it reaches us, and the peculiar circumstances under which it was given. What is the nature of these Seven Short Epistles of S. Ignatius? What were the circumstances under which they were written? What was the object of the writer in setting them forth? Let us bring S. Ignatius himself as a witness into court (I am speaking in the ears of men skilled in taking testimony, and who know the value of evidence), and let us examine him regarding his object in the writing of these letters—the time and the place when and where they were first given to the world. "What object had you, Ignatius, in the writing of these Epistles?" "I wrote them," he answers, "as simple letters, declaring what I found upon my journey from Antioch (of which city I was the Bishop) to Rome, where I was called to die for the truth, as it is in Jesus, in the ninth year of the reign of the Emperor Trajan, and the fortieth year of my Episcopate." "The journey from Antioch to Rome is a long one—what course did you take, and what incidents of importance befel you by the way?" "We took the usual route from Antioch to Seleucia, and proceeded thence by sea. We stopped to rest at Smyrna, and I was glad to avail myself of the opportunity to visit the holy Polycarp, then Bishop of the Smyrnaeans. Three of the neighboring Bishops, with their Presbyters and Deacons, when they heard of my arrival, came to see me, and I availed myself of the opportunity to send greeting to the Churches of Asia Minor." "Why did you write these letters to the Philadelphians, to the Magnesians, to the Trallians, and to the Church at Rome?" "I wrote them because the men who had me in their toils would not permit me to take these Churches in my way, and I was especially anxious that the brethren at Rome should not do anything to prevent my receiving the Crown of Martyrdom for which I longed." "Did you make any other stops besides that at Smyrna?" "Yes, we halted again at Troas, and there I had the chance to write to the Churches of Ephesus and Smyrna, and to Polycarp." "Who was this Polycarp, to whom you paid such honor and respect?" "Polycarp was, as I have said, Bishop of Smyrna, and he was the disciple of S. John, the last link in the line of the men of the past generation. He had been privileged to sit at the feet of the Beloved Disciple, and to hear from his own lips the things which had been taught him by his dear Lord and Master."

Such is the simple story of Ignatius and his journey to Rome. It will be observed that in writing his epistles, Ignatius was not writing a book to prove the existence of the Episcopate. He never thought of such a thing. There is no thought of controversy in his mind. He is upon a journey and he tells us in simple letters what he found upon his way. He gives you the names of the Churches, and he tells you that in every Church with which he was brought into contact in Asia Minor, he found existing Bishops, Priests, and Deacons. He gives you the names of the Churches and their Bishops. The Churches which he addresses (with the exception of Rome) had Ephesus for their centre. It was at Ephesus that S. John, the last of the Apostles, spent the last years of his life. He was left, while the others were taken away by violent deaths, that he might perfect the organization of the Church. He left behind him in Smyrna his disciple Polycarp. It was to Polycarp, Ignatius (who began the work of his ministry probably in the year 70 and carried it on for forty years, to the year 110) left the care of the Church of Antioch; and, as a successor of the apostles, gave it into his hands.

Take into consideration the whole of the circumstances connected with the writing of these Epistles of S. Ignatius, and you will agree with me, if I mistake not, in thinking that the evidence of such a witness to the existence of a threefold order of ministry in his day is indisputable and complete.

So much for the nature of the evidence itself. But why does Ignatius contend, as he confessedly does, for the divine origin of the Episcopate? Is he maintaining a theory? or is he dealing with a felt necessity, and an incontrovertible fact? The reason which Ignatius himself gives is that the existence of the Episcopate was necessary to the integrity of the faith, and to its perpetuation unadulterated to succeeding generations. The Episcopate, in the judgment of Ignatius, is the representative of the great principle of moral unity, and is accordingly the divinely ordained safeguard against all heretical pravity, and schismatical division in the family of God.

Let us look for a moment at the religious world as Ignatius found it in his day and generation. There were not less than some three hundred and sixty schools of thought in existence at the time. Nor were the philosophical teachers of the age mere dialecticians: they were moral teachers, and they professed to show men the way to lead a happier and a better life. Three hundred and sixty schools! One for every day in the year almost. But worse than the philosophers themselves, and more difficult to deal with, were the men who, under the names of Gnostics, or Rationalists, as we should call them now, sought to mingle together religion and philosophy, and set up schools and systems of their own to take the place of the Church of the Apostles. Now it is in opposition to these corrupters of the faith, Ignatius asserts the principle that Christianity is not an abstract or philosophical system, but involves in its very inception the idea of moral obedience. The doctrines of Christianity, he maintains, are neither more nor less than the logical exponents of its facts; and it is to the facts of the supernatural birth, and miraculous life, and atoning death of the Lord Jesus, that the apostles, and their successors in the Catholic Church (a phrase for the first time met with in the Epistles of S. Ignatius) were ordained to bear witness. It is not only, or chiefly, the truth of the doctrine that we have to consider (for that were to reduce Christianity to a speculative system), but primarily and first of all, we have to deal with the credibility and character of the witnesses. It was to bear *witness* that the apostles were chosen and set apart by Christ as the Sent of God; it was to perpetuate their testimony that the apostles, when called away, chose and set apart others to take their place. It will be seen at a glance, then, why Ignatius insists, as he does, upon obedience to the Bishop as the only true mark of Christian fellowship. It was not with him a question of mere truth and error—for there were many things which Christianity had in common with the schools of the philosophers—the real question at issue was, whether the professed teacher was an accredited witness to the truth as it had been received from the apostles, and was in possession of the due authority to educate and train up in the faith those who had been baptized into the name of Jesus. It was, in other words, a moral and historical question, involving habits of moral obedience and humility, and not a question of the reception of mere abstract truths and speculations. The Episcopate was the guardian of the faith, because it was the duly certified witness to the facts to which the apostles bore witness. It was not, it will be observed, a question of " tactual succession," as has been profanely said; nor was it a question of mere ecclesiastical arrangement; it was to the men of that age a question involving the credibility of witness, and the determination of the fact, whether the person professing to guide and to teach had entered in by the door, and was sent by the true Shepherd of the sheep; or had climbed up some other way, and had stamped upon him the brand of a thief and robber. A single illustration will make our meaning plain. The origin and nature of evil was one of the questions hotly disputed in the early days of Christianity, as it is now, and has been ever since. The Gnostic teachers of the time, without exception, held to the doctrine of dualism and the eternity of matter: this was the generally received doctrine of all philosophical schools, both East and West. Christianity too taught a belief in the existence of evil, but denied that Evil was eternal, or that it had any existence in itself apart from the Good. It was to meet this error of the Gnostic teachers of the age that the first article was inserted in the Creed, affirming the sovereign power of God the Father Almighty, and declaring Him to be the maker of all things both in heaven and earth. The article in the Creed was no empty profession of faith, it was no mere assertion of an abstract doctrine or belief. It had to be recited by every candidate for baptism, and was solemnly delivered to the catechumen, on the eve of their baptism, by the Bishop himself as the head of the congregation and the keeper of the faith. The faith then was not Embodied as it is now, a written formula, but was orally delivered by the living witness to the apostolic tradition ; and was openly confessed by the person seeking admission, before the whole Church. The bond between the recipient and the bestower was a living and personal bond, and of necessity involved living and personal relationships of loyalty and faith, and obedience to the authoritative witness to the belief of the Catholic Church, in opposition to the men who were tainted with the rationalism of the philosophic schools. In other words, in historical Christianity you cannot separate the faith, as it is authoritatively set forth in the Creed of the Church, from the teacher; and the teacher, in opposition to the many-voiced Babel of speculative rationalism, is, according to the teachings of the Epistles of S. Ignatius, the Bishop, as the representative of the moral unity of the whole body of the Church.

Will you say to me—This may all be true, but Gnosticism is a thing of the past; times differ, and men in the nineteenth century cannot be dealt with as men in the ninth century, and the primitive ages of the Church. I answer—The moral nature of man is the same in every age, requires the same spiritual remedies. Error now is the same as it was at first ; the name and the appearance may change, but the substance is the same. I hold in my hand a book entitled, "The Ten Religions of the World." It is written by one of the ablest representatives of modern thought, whose boast is that he is free from the trammels of tradition, and is in advance of the spirit of the past. What then does this teacher—who looks upon Christianity as another philosophy, and compares it with the religious systems of Confucius and Zoroaster, and Buddha—tell us about the problem of good and evil? What is his solution of the mystery; and how does it differ from the Rationalistic and Gnostic systems of the early days of Christianity? This then is the answer which James Freeman Clarke gives to the question, in the city of Boston, in the nineteenth century: "Some of the difficulties which we find in the actual constitution of things would be removed," he says, "if we accept the view that, while God is the creator and preserver of the universe as a whole, he has permitted beings inferior to himself, but vastly superior to man, to carry on the work of creation in subordination to his own universal laws. In a previous chapter we have seen how probable it is, that there is an immense hierarchy of intelligences extending upward from man toward God. Some of these may possess such large wisdom, such resources of reason, and insight as to be able, by making use of God's laws, to create new races of plants and animals such as we see in the earth. They would be creators under God just as man is a creator under God. Man's inventions are creations. Man has invented the plow, the pump, the carriage, the ship, by making himself acquainted with what we call the laws of nature. But these laws are only the ever-present agency of God. He fills all in all. He holds the universe in every atom by the mysterious power of gravitation. And though man, in his higher nature, derives his being directly from God, as the idea of right, of wrong, cause and effect, and the reason which contains the light of the infinite and eternal, testify, yet his lower bodily nature, by which he is allied to other animals, may have been gradually developed by the inventive powers of subordinate beings." It seems incredible, and yet it is true, that a professedly Christian teacher in the nineteenth century puts forth exactly the same theory of a Demiourgos or world-maker, to account for the mystery of evil, which the Gnostic teachers Saturninus, Basilides, and Valentinus of the first ages of the Church set forth in their day. It is a denial of the first article of the Christian faith, and is the very same "theory" of "the constitution of things" which that article was expressly framed to condemn. The writer doubtless would deny that he intended to contravene by his theory the fundamental verities of the Christian faith; but his denial does not affect the question that the dogmas of the Christian Church are one thing, the philosophical speculations of rationalistic teachers another and a very different thing—that there is no hope of return to Christian unity except on the bases of the Apostles' Creed, and the recognition of some properly constituted authority to set at naught the vain speculations of ignorant and foolish men. Nor let our object be mistaken in making such a claim. It is not the case that the Church has ever deliberately set out to make a creed, or has ever sought to impose her own arbitrary decrees upon the consciences of men. Had she been only left to do her proper work, the Church would gladly have rested in her implicit beliefs, and would willingly have been spared the trouble of calling her bishops from one end of the earth to the other to give explicit expression to the articles of her faith. It was unbelief, and the gainsaying of unlearned and foolish men, which compelled the Church to formulate the faith. There is not an article of the Creed which the Church has ever made out of whole cloth (if you will permit me so to speak). If the Church has ever formulated the faith, it was because she was forced so to do in opposition to the efforts made to draw men away from the simplicity and integrity of the faith into the acceptance of the fine-spun theories of the teachers of error. It is as true of every article of the Creed as it is of the first article, that it had its origin in some perversion of the faith; and it may with truth be affirmed that no person to-day is competent to give an intelligent opinion regarding the faith, as it is embodied in the Creed of the Church, who is ignorant of the nature of the error which it is the aim of the several articles to controvert. It is this that makes the work of Archbishop King upon the Creed of inestimable value to the proper understanding of the faith.

I have taken an illustration from the doctrinal and speculative sphere to prove the necessity that exists of our having recourse to the teaching and polity of the Apostolic Age, if we are ever to reach any sure basis for the restoration of the unity of Christendom. I shall now, with your permission, take another illustration from the liturgical and devotional sphere, in proof of a similar necessity, in things affecting the polity and practice of the Church. It was a surprise to many of us to hear, as we have lately been informed by a distinguished denominational teacher of our own city, that Easter—the glorious festival of the resurrection—is a compound of heathenism and Judaism, and is to be rejected by educated Christian men as a relic of the dark ages. It is surely to be regretted that, at a time when men would seem to be striving together in an effort to secure Christian unity, such a statement should have been made. If Easter-tide were only a religious sentiment, it might surely claim respectful consideration from all believing in the fact of the Resurrection; but when it is capable of proof, that the settlement of the Easter question in opposition to Judaism is one of the best attested facts of early, primitive Christianity, we can only wonder at the way in which religious prejudice can pervert the minds of men, and raise up barriers of separation which it is not even in the power of historical criticism to overcome. The early Church had its ritualistic controversies even as we have them now. The great question which agitated the Church, for the first three hundred years of its existence, was the proper time for the keeping of the Easter festival.

There was, in the Syrian church and in the churches of Asia Minor, a strong Ebionitish or Jewish party, made up chiefly of Hebrew converts and their sympathizers, who contended that the Christian church should follow the example of the Jewish church, and keep the great festival of Redemption on the 14th day of Nisan—the day of the Jewish passover—on whatever day of the week the 14th of Nisan might fall. There was much in favor of such a practice. On the other hand, there were reasons why the Christian feast should not be kept on the same day as the Jewish passover. It was desirable, in the first place, to draw as markedly as possible the line of difference between Judaism and Christianity. It was for this reason that Christians from the first did not keep the seventh day of the week as the day for their religious convocations; but the first day of the week—the day of the Resurrection. It was thought desirable also to give marked prominence to the truth, that Christianity is not only the completion of the old sacrificial and legal economy, but is also the beginning of a new economy—the entering in of a new life, and the setting up of a new kingdom in the world. And for this reason again, the feast ought to take place at the beginning of the week and not, in any case, toward its close. For three hundred years the fight went on between the Friday, as we may say, or the Sunday after. It was not an easy question to settle. Regard must be had to the prejudices of the Hebrew converts upon the one hand, and upon the other nothing must be left undone to assert the great principle that, in rising again from the dead our Lord rose as the head of the new creation, and the beginning of a new system of things: it was found necessary to symbolize the truth that the Church of Christ is above all else a Catholic Church which knows no people nor nationality, but accords equal privileges to Jew and to Greek, to barbarian and civilized, to bound and to free. We find the matter in dispute as early as the time of Polycarp, the disciple of S. John. Polycarp went to Rome to hold counsel about the matter with Anicetus. Polycarp contended that the churches of Asia Minor must be left to follow their own customs, which had been taught them, he said, by S. John when from Ephesus he ruled over the churches within his reach. The bishop of Rome agreed that it was best for the present that the East should follow its own traditions, and he allowed the venerable Polycarp to celebrate the Easter festival in the city of Rome after his own way.

But the lapse of time brought a change both in Asia Minor, and in Rome and the West. It is one thing to yield for the time being, in a conciliatory spirit, to the prejudiced and the weak; it is another, to sacrifice an important principle when the occasion has passed away for a reasonable demand for requiring the sacrifice. In the time of Victor it was felt that there was no reason why the East should continue any longer to differ from the West in keeping the Easter festival. Victor accordingly commanded Christians everywhere, on pain of excommunication, to keep the feast on the same Sunday, and not the exact day of the fourteenth of Nisan. Polycrates—at that time the successor of S. John in Ephesus—went up to Rome to defend the ancient privileges of the churches of Asia Minor, and to ask that their liberties, if not their prejudices, should be considered in the matter. The spirit of Victor was different from that of Anicetus, and he refused to yield any longer in the point at issue. When Irenaeus, who was himself from Asia Minor, and had succeeded Pothinus in Gaul, heard of the action of Victor of Rome, he wrote to him and begged of him not to divide the Church for such a trifling question as the day for celebrating the Easter festival. Victor yielded, and the threatened excommunication was suspended. It is not, then, the case that the Easter festival of the Christian Church is a compound of Judaism and Paganism. The reverse of this, as the facts of the case prove, is true.

But the controversy has an interest for us over and above its ritualistic value. It confirms the principle which the Anglican Church has always maintained in its controversy with Rome. We take our stand to-day on precisely the same ground which Polycarp and Polycrates did, as to the right of a national church to order its own internal affairs without any breach of unity. As to the great outlying body of Protestantism, we have no wish to revive past controversies; or to deal with the questions at issue in any other spirit than that of love and Christian charity. Our prayer is that God, in His own good time, will reunite again divided Christendom in one fold, under one Shepherd. It is not a question of mere ecclesiastical arrangement, much less of worldly power; it is a practical question to which history and experience bear witness. In unity there is strength; in division and strife, ruin and loss. We only repeat the words of the Master when we affirm that " if a house be divided against itself that house cannot stand." If it be true that, if Satan be divided against Satan, his kingdom cannot stand, it is likewise true that God cannot be divided against Himself. He is a lover of unity, and not the author of confusion. Why do we want *organic* unity? We want it for the reason that it is necessary for the preservation of the faith, even as it is for the development and growth of the life of the Church. Without it the Church has no power to contend with the world, or to withstand the disintegrating forces of self-will and heretical tendencies among her own children. The remark of Guizot regarding the fifth century is also true when applied to the nineteenth century. Had it not been for the organism of the Christian Church, Guizot tells us, the world must have perished and the social fabric suffered utter disintegration when the Roman Empire was crushed under the feet of the barbarians.

Had Christianity then been a thing of mere individual feeling, and not, as it was, a great social power knit together by joints and bands, it never could have risen above the wreck of the nations of the earth when the Goths took possession of the empire. "Humanly speaking," Guizot says, "it was the Christian Church that saved Christianity; . . it was the Christian Church, with its institutions, its magistrates, its authority; the Christian Church which struggled so vigorously to prevent the interior dissolution of the empire, which struggled against barbarism, and, in fact, overcame the barbarian; it was the Church . . . which became the great connecting link—the principle of civilization between the Roman and the barbarian world." The verdict of history we claim is, that there must be in the world some abiding power, some organic agency above that of mere individualism, or else society will go to ruin. Represent it by what formula you may, the idea of moral unity for which Ignatius in his day contended, and the Church of England fought in her struggle with non-conformity, is essential to the very idea of the Church, and is the only spiritual force which can knit together into one the divided members of Christendom.

The North African Church and its Teachers.

LECTURE III.

REV. J. F. GARRISON, D.D.,

Professor of Liturgics in the Divinity School, Philadelphia.

THE NORTH AFRICAN CHURCH AND ITS TEACHERS.

THE subject of this lecture is The North African Church and its Teachers, with special reference to "a basis for the reunion of Christendom."

From the changes that have occurred in the scenes and nationalities of history, it may seem strange to many of the present day to hear that North Africa had ever played a prominent part in the progress of the Church, or had been profoundly related to the development of our modern civilization. For centuries past Morocco, Algiers, Tunis, Tripoli, and the states contiguous to them on the Northern African shore of the Mediterranean Sea, have been known to Europe and America only by the worthlessness and viciousness of a marauding, piratical population; and the conquest and annexation of several of these countries as provinces by France and Italy has been regarded as equally a benefit to the people whom they have conquered, and a relief to the commerce of the Mediterranean from their constant annoyance and pillage.

But it was far otherwise in the days of the later Roman Republic, and even (though with widely different conditions) under the Empire for four hundred years and more after the beginning of the Christian era.

In its prime North Africa was the seat of Carthage, the home of the mightiest enemy that the Republic of Rome ever knew, and although subdued and destroyed as an independent power and a rival, it had revived from its ashes and was one of the most populous and important provinces of the later Republic and the Empire. And Carthage, now transformed in all respects into a Roman city, was second throughout the whole West only to Rome itself in elegance, culture, population, and display.

The area of North Africa as a proconsular jurisdiction was somewhat over two thousand miles in length, with an average breadth of about three hundred miles between the sea and the desert. From its location and climate, this province had become one of the chief granaries whence Rome and Italy drew their supplies of food, and as a consequence, its territory was occupied by a wealthy and prosperous people. It was dotted along all its sea-coast with large and elegant cities, and towns of no mean pretensions abounded in every part of the province.

Christianity must have been introduced into North Africa very early, and with great success; for when it first comes to the notice of history, its adherents were already exceedingly numerous, and everywhere, throughout the province, they had long been organized into dioceses and local parishes, and constituted a compact and efficient power in every important city and town.

The period at which the North African Church thus first appears in history, was about the year 200, or a little before; and it continued to play a most distinguished part in the thought and life of the Church, until about the middle of the fifth century, when, with all of the Western Empire, it was buried and for a while almost forgotten under the successive waves of the Barbarians. This period of two hundred and fifty years during which the North African Church is prominent, was marked and spanned by the lives of three of the most renowned teachers of the Western Church. These three men were Tertullian, with whom the period begins; Cyprian, who marks about its middle; and Augustine, with whom it comes to its close.

The North African Church, at the time of its greatest prosperity, numbered some four hundred and sixty dioceses in union with the Catholic Church and under its authority; while there was an almost equal number of bishops who ruled over the congregations of an extensive and disastrous schism, which for a long period prevailed in North Africa, and is known in ecclesiastical history as Donatism.

This has seemed to many so extravagantly large a number as to be almost incredible. But so populous and rich was the country in these centuries, that Bingham asserts there could have been an average of seventy or eighty large towns and villages to each diocese of the Catholic Bishops, and that the geographical area of the several jurisdictions would, on the same average, be about one-half that of the ordinary French diocese of to-day.

The first of the three great teachers by whom the African Church was made illustrious was, as already said, Tertullian; and it is with his writings, his public life, and his surroundings, from A.D. 192 to 220 or 225, that we must begin. Septimius Florens Tertullianus was born in Carthage about A.D. 150 or 160. His family were pagans, his father an officer in the Imperial army, evidently a man of means, able and willing to give his son the best education that the times could afford him. The lad was familiar with the poetry, and learned in the philosophy and history of the great Greek masters, and himself both talked and wrote the Greek. He seems to have been trained especially for the profession of a lawyer, and became famous in his early manhood for his knowledge of the Roman Law and his ability as an advocate.

As he was not converted until near middle life (thirty-five or forty) and his family were heathens, he was fully acquainted with the scenes and influences of the theatre and the arena, and shared more or less the dissipation and profligacy which then marked so much of the social life of the heathen. He was thus early familiar, by his own experience, with the very evils and sins of which in his maturer life he was to be so stern a censor; he was also furnished, by the wide range of his studies and his own elaborate and careful mental training, with the weapons of which he made so powerful a use in his after-years of Christian teaching and controversy.

Doubtless also, being a North African, he inherited by birth, like many other of the Carthaginian families, traits derived from the fierce, fiery peoples who were the ancient inhabitants of Carthage. And after his conversion he devoted himself to the defence of Christianity, as he understood it, in precisely the spirit with which Hamilcar swore his son Hannibal, upon the altar of the gods, to an eternal and implacable hostility and warfare with Rome.

But Tertullian was not only the first of the illustrious leaders of the North African Church, he was also, what is vastly more important, the first of the great Latin writers and teachers of the Church of the West.

Christianity, the Church, both had their origin and found their early home in the East. They belonged to Asia, to Palestine, and Syria, not to Europe. The language too, the Greek, in which their sacred records were written, although in name European, had virtually become, since the conquest of Alexander, an Oriental language; and in the time of the Apostles was, as it continued for a long period after, the common medium of literary intercourse for all Asia from the Euphrates to the Mediterranean; and was used by all the cultivated thinkers of Alexandria and Egypt. It was this prominent position of the Greek in this age which caused all the authoritative scriptures of the Church to be written in that language; and it seems also to have led certain of the portions of the Church, where the Greek was not thus familiar to the people, to allow it for a time to restrain them from the use of their own tongue in their writings or discussions on matters relating to Christianity.

The preaching of the Gospel was extended to Rome and other parts of the West before the death of S. Peter and S. Paul. But while the Church was thus extended very early into the West, and grew very rapidly in all the western provinces of the Roman Empire, which we now know as England, France, Spain, Italy, and North Africa, it is a fact to be noted as a consequence of the influences already mentioned, that from the foundation of the Church to the end of the third century, with rare exceptions, all the great works on Theology as well as the universal creeds of the Church had been produced in the East—in Syria, Asia Minor, or Alexandria— and were all written in Greek.

During all this long period, when the Church was discussing with intense zeal the new conceptions about God and man which the revelations of the

Gospel had awakened in men, when the Christian world was struggling with eager desire to comprehend the most fully and express the most clearly, the great doctrines which were to constitute its future Theology and the forms of the creeds in which these should be embodied for all after-ages, during all this long and vitally important period of three hundred years, in which the foundations of Christian philosophy and Christian theology were being laid you may question the whole line of the Bishops of Rome and not find one really able or noteworthy contribution to the vast work which was being done by the Church in the East and in the Greek language. Nor had the rest of the Church in Western Europe been greatly more active in this work of the early ages of Christianity than the Bishops and Clergy of Rome. Irenæus and Hippolytus had both written notable works, and on matters of considerable moment in the history of the Church, and they both lived in the West; but notwithstanding this, the language of all their known writings was Greek, and wellnigh all that makes these of real value came to them from their early and intimate acquaintance with the thoughts and modes of expression, as well as the language and church literature, of the East.

The only real exceptions to this, not very creditable, lack in the Western Church, were in North Africa. It is to Tertullian (about A.D. 200) we must give the high place of being first in the series of great teachers of Christianity who afterward wrote in Latin. And, although there was no adequate treatment of theology as a whole in the West until two hundred and fifty years later, in the writings of Augustine, yet in Tertullian we have the beginning of a true Western theology, presented too, for the first time, in forms of thought familiar to the West, and in a language known to that portion of the Church.

The condition of the heathen world in Tertullian s age, and the necessities of the Western or Latin-speaking Church, both called imperatively for this phase of Christian teaching, and his character and training, as we have already traced them, were such as eminently fitted him to begin the work.

The life-force of the old civilizations East and West, Gaul, Rome, and Africa, as well as Greece, Syria, and Egypt, was utterly exhausted; the old religious faiths were dead; their outer forms had continued only as state ceremonials to please the mob, or from a grovelling superstition which feared some unknown evil if it should abandon them; the old systems of philosophy were powerless for any other use than mere word play or a pretence of erudition; the only school in the pagan world that then or afterward made any impression on the minds of men was that known as the Alexandrian or new Platonic philosophy. No greater name had appeared among the Greek thinkers, since the days of Plato and Aristotle, than its brilliant master Plotinus. The system he taught in Rome soon after the death of Tertullian—and as if to present the best that was possible in Heathen thought in rivalry with the beginning of the new life that had come from the Gospel—was of rare beauty, sublimity, and excellence. Yet so wholly unable were the old lines of thought to retain their power over the mind of the world, that its momentary flash of splendor was only that of a sun illumining the clouds behind which it was soon to sink in darkness and forever.

With the breaking up of the old religions and old philosophies had come also the loss of all the accustomed restraints of the moral and social customs which belonged to them. The conquest of all nations had made Rome and her near provinces the centre of the conquered world. She brought their innumerable gods to the imperial city and set them in the Pantheon. She dragged her captives there as slaves, and spread them broadcast by the millions over Italy and Africa. Degraded by their slavery and desperate in their wretchedness, these miserables in every sense sought only to curry favor with their masters by pandering to every vice and mingling into one horrid slough the infamies, the crimes, the debaucheries of every people.

The lords of the far provinces, or Roman officials (corrupted by residing there), flocked also around the capital, each rivalling the other in extravagance of display and in unnamable, almost unthinkable pollution of themselves and all who came in contact with their vileness.

Gibbon says (111, 112): "The capital attracted all the vices of the universe. The intemperance of the Goths, the cunning of the Greeks, the savage obstinacy of the Egyptians and Jews, the servile temper of the Asiatics, the effeminate prostitution of the Syrians," all were commingled in this various multitude. It was an age, too, of luxury and extravagance of living which we, with all our conceptions of millionaires and expenditure, can hardly reproduce even in imagination. It was a time also of high art, at least if art consist, as some appear to think, in painting all that can inflame the passions, and suggest evil to the mind, instead of that which seeks to give expression to the true, and pure, and noble as essential elements of beauty. Art was seen everywhere; the walls were alive with pictures —outside as well as in—the floor as often as the ceiling.

So also literature (such as it was) abounded; perhaps books never were so numerous or so universally read in any age or part of the world, except in the last century or two, as in the period of which we speak. Yet, with all these elements of culture, these agencies of "sweetness and light" which so many now believe to be the needed new gospel for the race, literature, art, the cosmopolite mingling of all nations, and all faiths and no faith in any, so far were they from humanizing and beautifying society and life, that earth never saw such inhumanity and brutalizing cruelty as marked these centuries in the great cities of the Roman Empire and certain of its provinces; cruelty too, without reason, without even the excuse of fanaticism or hate; cruelty solely, simply because all moral and religious bonds once cast aside, the brute in his ravening, starved moods, becomes the man.

The Roman lady had her slave maid (often a captive reared in her far off home as delicately as herself) stand as she made her toilet with bared shoulders, that the thongs of the angry mistress, tipped with iron, might cut more surely into the blood for every slight mistake. Men racked their serfs with pitiless vengeance on any occasion, or even without occasion, whenever the passion of a cruel master inflamed him to brutality, or the fears of a timid tyrant impelled him to a course of terrorism. Men and women, ten, fifty, or eighty thousand of them, would sit in the amphitheatre day after day, week after week, to gaze on the ferocious combats of wild beasts one with another; or, when satiated with what had now become the dull monotony of a death-fight between tigers, they desired a keener stimulus would call for men to fight each other—men not allowed clothing, that the death-wounds might be more easily given—who fought, each murdering and murdered until there were none left who could murder or be murdered. Nor was this all. In the time of Tertullian it was no uncommon thing for the wild cry of the mob to call out " The Christians to the lions ! The Christians to the lions ! "—and in this very city of Carthage, in the very amphitheatre where Tertullian had sat (as he shudderingly tells us) in his early years, two delicate young mothers, Perpetua and Felicitas, scarce out of their teens, were dragged into the arena before the bloodthirsty throng and tossed on the horns of mad wild cattle, until the soldiers, in pure mercy, ended their appalling agonies with the sword; and perhaps the most terrible sentence in the whole frightful narrative, written, too, in all probability by Tertullian himself, is " the populace called for them (when about to receive their death-stroke) to come into the middle of the arena, that, as the sword penetrated their body, they (the multitude) might make their eyes partners in the murder."

It was into the old world thus debauched, soulless, and degraded, with all its refinement and culture, thus effeminate, cowardly, and cruel, notwithstanding its high art and universal literature, that Tertullian was born. And it was from this (and with a thorough knowledge of its mingled splendor and vileness) that, about his fortieth year, he was converted to Christianity and baptized into the Church.

We know not whether this great revolution in his life was made at Carthage or Rome, but we know, from what has already been shown of him, that he did nothing by halves. When he had once seized the divine significance and worth of Christianity, he gave himself to it with all his intense nature and all his large acquirements; and from the beginning it so possessed his entire being that he saw nothing in the whole world worth a thought, nothing worth having or worth living for, but the Gospel. And even while yet a layman he wrote (both for the heathen in defence of Christianity and on special matters of Christian interest) several of the most valuable of his numerous writings. One of those, known as "The Apology," presents with wonderful power the contrast between the Christian and pagan life and principles; in this occurs the famous passage so often misquoted as " the blood of the martyrs is the seed of the Church." He says to the rulers of Rome, " Go on, zealous governors, sacrifice the Christians at the will of the people, kill us, torture us, condemn us, grind us to dust, your cruelty will not avail you; the oftener we are mown down by you, the more in number we grow; the Blood of Christians is seed."

It was inevitable, also, that the same temperament would demand from his fellow-Christians the most uncompromising and rigid following of what he thought to be the consistent life of the Christian.

Unhappily, notwithstanding the dangers by which the Christians were constantly surrounded, many who were members of the Church winked at, or even shared in, acts which were unworthy of their profession, and others (while not doing anything positively evil) were treading in paths which he felt would lead to sin. Not only was he sorely grieved at these inconsistencies, but at the same time a portion of the clergy assumed airs of pretension and superiority, and by their insolence or display aroused his personal indignation. In the one case as well as the other, we may readily believe that neither his tongue nor his pen was idle in reproving conduct which he thought to be so opposed to the lofty ideal which the Christian life required.

While in this condition of mind he came in contact with a class of teachers recently come from Asia, known in Church history as Montanists, from the name of their chief—Montanus. The tenets of this system, or at least some of them, seemed to meet precisely the necessities of the position he occupied. Without going into the details of these, it is sufficient for our purposes to know that, as he understood or modified them, they maintained that the Church needed (after Christ) a special dispensation of the Holy Ghost as essential to its continuance and advance; that certain persons (Montanus, their chief) were possessed of such light; that it was by this Light the individual Christian must be constantly led in the directing of his own Christian life and conduct; and that such persons must be regarded as actual organs of the Holy Ghost, who spake by them as his agents in the guidance of the Church. They held that the articles of essential faith had been established once for all, hence these could not be changed. But for the present needs of the Church and of its members, such personal utterances of the

Divine Spirit were essentially necessary. How much of the real Montanism Tertullian accepted is not known, but he was supremely convinced of its central idea, which in its essence was very much the same as the Quakerism of George Fox—the vital necessity of conscious personal relations to the Holy Spirit as above any mere external authority or ordinary Church legislation, for the correct understanding and direction of the Christian individual or the Church as a whole.

Neither the opinions of Tertullian on such a matter, nor his mode of presenting them were, as we may well believe, such as would be acceptable to the authorities of the Church, and (whether by his own act or that of the authorities is not important) he left the communion of the Church, though he still continued the vigorous use of his pen and voice upon whatever question of Christian interest he felt himself called to speak. Neither is it certain whether he remained apart from the Catholics or returned to their communion late in life, as he soon disappears from the view of history, and we know really nothing of his later years.

But whichever was the case, it is quite certain that the Church as a whole has always ranked him among her most distinguished "Fathers;" and notwithstanding his relations with the Montanist Schism, he has occupied a higher place and exercised a far wider influence as one of the great Leaders of Christian thought than most of those who have been officially recognized as saints and enrolled as Doctors of the Church.

Turning now from the character and work of Tertullian, as a man and a Presbyter dealing with the personal life of the Christian, what do his writings afford directly or incidentally as "a basis for the reunion of Christendom?"

I must assume here, what has been fully treated in the preceding Lectures, that nothing should be deemed essential in a basis for Christian Union—at least intercommunion—that was not accepted and acted upon by the Church Catholic as fundamental in the belief or organization of the early centuries; and conversely, that whatever of either faith or order was in these same centuries universally recognized and enforced as fundamental, cannot safely be disregarded in any basis for a reunion of Christendom in our day.

On the great issues of the vital truths of the Creed, the Divineness and Authority of Holy Scriptures, the obligations and benefits of the two Sacraments, there was no question as to their Catholic authority then and, happily, none in their acceptance by wellnigh all societies which are called churches at the present time.

But on one of the matters which have been largely the subject of controversy, much light emerges in connection with his discussions of the various heresies which were then disturbing the peace of the Church, this is the question of the

"Historic Episcopate." Certain heretical teachers had set up a wholly new idea of Christ, one differing widely from that held by the Church; they claimed that their conception was the true representation of the actual Christ, and was to be accepted instead of that which the Church maintained. Among other grounds on which they rested their new theories was the authority of Holy Scripture, and one of their most effective modes of argument was the quotation of certain passages from the Bible, mainly the New Testament; these they interpreted by rules of their own making, and then applied them to the support of the opinions they sought to promulgate.

Tertullian entered very early, and with great vigor, into the contest with these Heretics—Gnostics, as they were called—but his line of argument was wholly different from theirs; he believed in Holy Scripture as thoroughly as they, and quoted it as confidently; but, since their method left each party to fix its own sense on every passage and on its meaning as a whole, there was no end to the discussion; it was a mere word-battling as to whose interpretation was the better; there could be no positive ground for decision either way; hence Tertullian brings in another witness, but one whose testimony could be very easily overthrown if open to denial, yet very decisive if in itself undeniable. It is virtually: "Your doctrine is not scriptural, is not from or of the Apostles who wrote the Scriptures, because in every great city, in every part of the Empire, there are at this time Bishops who can, each one of them (from the records, etc., of his Diocese), trace back his predecessors to the time of the Apostles, and the first of these in every line received his authority and his doctrine from the Apostles or their companions; now, all these men, thus receiving and handing down the Apostolic Truth (*i.e.*, Bible Teaching), agree in the same great essentials of Doctrine, and no one of them ever, until your heresy, heard of your opinions or beliefs. Hence, as they have continued in unbroken succession from the beginning, to teach and hand down the truths they learned from the Apostles as well as the Scriptures written and authorized by the Apostles, and are now all in agreement as to the great Doctrines of the Bible and the Church, their teaching must be regarded as the true Doctrine of the Apostles and the Holy Word."

The reply to this (if false) would have been very obvious, very easily applied, thoroughly crushing. All that would be needed was to assert, on evidence that could not have been difficult to find, " your statement is not true, your line of Bishops in this city began only fifty years ago, that in Jerusalem commenced with a man who never saw an Apostle; or, if you can trace something back one hundred years, it had no authority, and here and there are scores of cities with many churches, and they have not, and never had, any such succession as your

Bishops." The assertion of the existence of such a series of lines, their succession, their authority, was open to disproval by a cloud of witnesses over all the Church.

And yet, with all the ability, the zeal, the acuteness of the Heretics, we find no hint of any such endeavor; there is abundance of keen, subtle, often powerful, reasoning, but nowhere any effort to deny this potent evidence from history; the facts then, as facts, may fairly be considered as beyond any serious contradiction. But if accepted as facts, they draw with them at least one conclusion, *i.e.*, that in the second century it was universally admitted, by Heretic and Orthodox alike, that Bishops each descended in a line beginning from the Apostles, appointed and authorized directly or mediately by them, were an integral element of the organization of the Christian Church as left by the Apostles, and hence must be retained as fundamental in any proposal looking to the reunion of Christendom on an historical and apostolic basis.

There is another point (in quite an opposite direction) on which the testimony of Tertullian comes with effective weight; this is, that the Church in the third century did not hold either the infallibility or supreme authority of the Bishop of Rome. He was, from the very position of his city, the chief Bishop of the West; the general belief that S. Peter and S. Paul were both martyred at Rome, had invested its church and head with high veneration, the succession of its Bishops, although none of them had as yet made any contributions to the theology of the Church, had nevertheless been mostly composed of shrewd, wise, able men, and they had done a mighty work in organizing and unifying the Western Church. For all these reasons, the Roman Bishop had been regarded from an early date as the Patriarch of the West, and also as being in an especial sense the successor there of S. Peter. On the other hand, a See recognized as entitled to so distinguished a position, would be under constant temptation to add to its distinction and importance, by ever-increasing claims of superiority, and, whenever it seemed possible, to introduce and enforce its own authority and jurisdiction in other portions of the Church. Such was the course of Rome, but the North African Church never, in any period of its existence as a separate church, admitted the exercise of any such authority or rule; on the contrary, its leaders were always prompt (when they thought the occasion called for it) to repudiate the assumption of the Roman Bishop, to charge and to reprove his errors whether of belief or conduct, to treat him indeed as a distinguished fellow-Bishop, whom they were ready to honor because of his high station, but (as S. Paul said to the followers of Peter in Galatia) "to whom they gave place by subjection—no, not for an hour" (Gal. 2, 5).

In a certain matter on which Tertullian felt very deeply, the Bishop of Rome had declared that absolution should be given for certain sins for which Tertullian thought it ought not to be allowed; hence in a tract discoursing of the subject, the fiery North African condemns both the opinion and expression of the Roman Bishop with indignant sarcasm, "I hear there has been an edict set forth; the Supreme Pontifex"—(the very term was contemptuous, very much as we now say "the Great Mogul," as the title was at this time, and for two centuries after, exclusively appropriated to the Roman Emperor, hence was applied here to the Roman Bishop only in derision)—"The Supreme Pontifex the Bishop of Rome issues an edict; O Edict, on which cannot be inscribed 'good deed,' Far, far from Christ's betrothed (the Church) be such proclamation; She does not make it; if because the Lord said to Peter, 'to Thee I have given the key,' etc., etc., you presume that this power has derived to you, what sort of a man are you, subverting and changing the manifest intention of the Lord, which conferred this gift personally on Peter?" And he goes on to show how it was fulfilled in the life and person of Peter himself, but that it conveyed no such power to his successors in the Episcopate, and most assuredly none to the Bishop of Rome upon any ground whatever.

If this opinion of Tertullian stood alone in the history of the African Church, it might be regarded as only the utterance of an individual who thus felt; but it becomes an invaluable testimony that submission to, or recognition of, the authority of Rome was not an accepted doctrine of the early ages, when we find, as will be shown later on, that it was likewise repudiated both by individuals and councils of the North Africans, continuously, for more than two hundred years from the time of Tertullian.

Accordingly, as not being a part of either the doctrine or the practice of the Primitive Church, it cannot enter into a basis for the reunion of Christendom to-day.

While Tertullian was in the height of his fame and his labors (about A.D. 200), was born, probably in or near Carthage, Thascius Cyprian, the second of the splendid trio of North African teachers.

He was also, like Tertullian, trained in all the learning and culture of the educated Roman of his time. He was an orator by profession, and a teacher of rhetoric. His wealth was ample, he lived in elegance, and enjoyed through all his life the companionship of the men of the highest rank in Roman society and in the state.

He was not converted until well on in middle life, somewhere between forty and forty-five. He had been so highly esteemed by all the people of Carthage, while yet a heathen, that very soon after his baptism (and not in literal accordance with the canons) he was called—almost compelled—by the Christians in Carthage to be made priest, and almost immediately after was consecrated as their Bishop.

This rapid elevation to the Episcopate seemed at the time to be, and perhaps (in the then condition of that Church) was, fully justifiable and right; but it was not so regarded by all the clergy of the province, and it originated a faction hostile to Cyprian, which remained an unceasing source of annoyance and hindrance to him through all his after-life. In the main outlines of his theology he was largely influenced by Tertullian. He may well have heard his great fellow-countryman preach, he was thoroughly familiar with all his writings, and was constantly accustomed to call him his master and teacher (Magister).

But, as a Bishop of so prominent a city as Carthage he was called, from the stormy and terrible condition of his age and of the Church, to deal chiefly with urgent and perilous public questions involving the interests of the Church as a whole. A distinguished French writer* says of him: "Around him turns the whole Catholic organization of his age; he is its director and master;" he directs "how best to encourage the feeble, to moderate the violent, to call back the apostates, to quiet the people, to maintain due obedience; what a wonderful union of heroic faith and assiduous prudence could alone guide aright that grand work, which at the same time embraced life and death, this world and eternity; he was a great administrator and a statesman of the very highest order."

* Chasles: Études sur les premiers temps du Christianisme, etc.

The persecutions in North Africa, which seem to have relaxed for some years after Tertullian's death, broke out with new fury soon after the accession of Cyprian to the Episcopate. And they brought with them numerous complications the most puzzling and difficult, both in the personal relations of Cyprian and in his official action as Bishop.

When this storm first fell upon Carthage, Cyprian thought it best for his work and the Church that he should withdraw for a time from the city and live in retirement. Undoubtedly this was then the wise, right course to take (as the result fully justified). Although removed from immediate danger, he still directed with consummate judgment, ability, and tact all the affairs of his diocese, and discussed with recognized wisdom many of the vital and yet perplexing problems which the New Life of the Church was every day called on to meet in other portions of the Christian world.

After about fourteen months the Bishop returned to Carthage, but it was only to find yet more troublesome issues forced upon him while the difficulties of his position were greatly increased by the malignant strictures on his fleeing from martyrdom, made by the faction opposed to him.

One of the most puzzling of these issues (especially under his circumstances) arose from the excessive veneration of the Christians for those who had suffered in the persecution, *i.e.*, Christians who were waiting in prison in the expectation of death, or who were at the time actually suffering from torture, starvation, or wasting decay as slaves in the metal mines.

It was felt by all hearts that these were sacrificed heroes of the faith, and they were regarded by the Christian community with a reverence and devotion almost without limit. It is a cold heart indeed that (even after so many centuries) can read with undimmed eye the piteous stories of their sufferings and their bravery. One of their number (confessors, as they were called) writes to another the fate of a few of their common acquaintance. It is a bare catalogue for brevity, and yet opens a vista of unspeakable horrors. " Bassus is in the metal mines. Mappalicus under torture. Fortunio in the dungeon. Paulus has been tortured. Victor, Julia (and several others) were put to death in prison by hunger. In a few days you will hear that I have died the same." And in reply the friend to whom he writes, tells him of " the brave Saturninus, who would not abjure Christ even when they tore him with pincers of iron." We cannot wonder that the fellow-Christians of men and heroic women such as these should have rendered them a love hardly short of adoration.

On the other hand, it is a strange (though perhaps natural) exhibition of human nature, that many of these confessors so sublime in endurance, so unmoved before death, were yet so elated and puffed up with the reverence and adulation given them, that they came to deem themselves superior to all the order, discipline, and law of the Church; and to believe that they possessed supreme power to arrest its penalty on anyone who was under discipline, or to restore to full membership by their word whatever apostate or other offender would come to them for absolution. To all such they gave a certificate or little book, which demanded of the Bishop that he should at once reinstate its bearer and accept as final the absolution of the confessors.

It needs no explanation to show the innumerable, disastrous evils which must result from such an utter destruction of all the safeguards and barriers both of morals and government. And yet so blind was the devotion of the mass of the people to the Holy Confessors, that only a man of Cyprian's consummate ability could have guided the Church safely through such a perilous strait.

I cannot pause here to give even an outline of the long and bitter struggle that grew out of this, nor of the wise judgment which shaped the course of Cyprian. Suffice it to say that he settled the principle for all after-time, "that the Church must be governed and discipline ministered by the legal authority and according to law, not on the personal impulses of even the most holy, or the independent action of even the most meritorious."

There were other questions in which he was interested, which have more definite bearing on the basis for the reunion of Christendom.

The first was, whether baptism performed by others than ministers of the Orthodox Catholic Church was valid—or ought to be repeated? Cyprian zealously contended that such baptisms had no value, were in fact not Christian baptism at all; hence all who came into the Church having this only, must be re-baptized, or rather then first receive true baptism. But in this he, and those influenced by him, were opposed to almost all the rest of the Church, and to the ancient usage and tradition of the greater portion of the Church, which had always held that "a baptism with water, with Christ's appointed formula 'In the name of the Father, and of the Son, and of the Holy Ghost,' was a true baptism and ought not to be repeated." His opposition to this did not prevail, and the Church has always held that such baptisms were valid, and all such persons are baptized. Hence this need not stand in the way of a reunion. And the Church can cordially recognize all who have been thus baptized as true members of the body of Christ; that is, as being already members of the Catholic Church, and needing only to be restored to the communion of her apostolic form.

The second question above referred to was his relation as Bishop to the Bishop of Rome.

In the discussion of baptism, as on several other questions, he had differed very widely from the Bishop who at the time occupied the See of Rome. Upon certain of these questions the Roman Bishop had spoken in a tone which savored, in the opinion of Cyprian, too much of authority; in response, upon more than one occasion, the Bishop of Carthage not only "differs from his dear brother of Rome" (whom he also addresses as "his colleague") in most emphatic language, but even declares him wholly in error; and while reproving, as he terms it, "the bitter obstinacy of our Brother Stephen," he rather wonders "whether an account can be satisfactorily rendered in the day of Judgment for a priest who maintains the opinion, which his dear brother had announced and approved."

He willingly admits, as did all the Western Church, the primacy and honor of the Bishop of Rome (he was not known as The Pope for some three or more centuries after this), but he adds, immediately after asserting this, that the rest of the apostles were also (the same as Peter) endowed with a like partnership both of honor and power. Nor did Cyprian and North Africa stand alone in the expression of like views in this same period; among the correspondents of Cyprian was a Bishop of Asia, one Firmilian, who says in reference to the course of the Roman Bishop: "Those who are at Rome vainly pretend the authority of the Apostles" in the claims they make for their decisions on points of doctrine. "Stephen (Bishop of Rome) has dared to depart from the peace and unity of the Church," "and he has rebelled against the sacrament and the faith with contumacious discord."

It needs no argument to show that, with such opinions and expressions as these, neither the infallibility nor the supremacy of the Roman Bishop could have been regarded in that age as an essential of either belief or practice in the Catholic Church, and hence cannot be required as conditions in any basis of reunion now.

In the third of the subjects mentioned, Cyprian gives what he really did hold as the Apostolic Catholic teaching on the constitution and order of the Church. He seems to have formed his opinions on this very early in his ministry; but these were first given in their completed form in the immortal treatise entitled on "The Unity of the Church," and read as a sort of charge to a council at Carthage after his return from his exile during the first persecution. Here, as elsewhere, he maintains that the unity of the Church was symbolized in Peter; but, as before stated, in conjunction with this he also declares that a partnership in power and honor was also given to all the apostles, and that the principle of this unity was that "The whole episcopate is one undivided body, of which each Bishop holds a part (as a member) for the whole." "The Bishop is in the Church and the Church in the Bishop;" hence no Bishop is or can be, as Bishop, supreme over any other. In connection with this he, again and again, asserts that each Bishop is and must be independent in his own jurisdiction; accordingly he tells his dear brother in

Rome, "Each prelate has in the administration of his own church the exercise of his free will, as he shall give account to God;" and elsewhere he writes, "Every Bishop disposes and directs his own acts," etc.

The independence, however, thus maintained by Cyprian did not mean that each Bishop was wholly irresponsible to the Church for what he taught, and in the conduct of the Diocese. His own expression of the need of unity and his personal action unite to show that he had an entirely different intention; the Bishops were free from subserviency one to another, or to any one Bishop as supreme over all the others. But as a corporate unity, a whole of which each held an equal part with all the others, and for the good of all, they were all responsible to the control of the organic whole; and this was effected (following the examples of the apostles at Jerusalem) by the council or synod of the province, or of the whole church, by which that whole was represented and through which it acted.

It was not yet the time for the great General Councils; Nice was not convened till nearly seventy years after Cyprian; but from the beginning of his Episcopate he had recognized the full significance of the council, and so constantly had he called his brethren of North Africa together for decision and co-operation, that the use of the Council was virtually established on its proper basis by his administration. Councils had always been an essential element in the working of the Church, but he first developed their full effectiveness and influence; and when the Universal Councils came, the Church had already learned (mainly from Cyprian) to recognize in them the right and sufficient means whereby the Bishops, in their several jurisdictions, were enabled to be as they should be, independent one of another, and yet the unity of the Church, as one divine whole, be maintained by the Council, the common voice of all.

An universal episcopacy handed down from the Apostles, in which each Bishop has an independent authority, but under responsibility to God, and the voice of the Church as an organic whole expressed through its councils, was undoubtedly the belief of Cyprian and the entire Church Catholic of his age. As such it would need very strong opposing testimony to reject this from the principles that were deemed fundamental in the organization of the Apostolic Church.

Although Cyprian had avoided the first persecution, yet the time came at length when he himself felt that the sacrifice now asked of him was to give his life for the Church. Another persecution was ordered, especially of the Bishops and chief leaders of the Christians. For a while Cyprian was only banished by the government from Carthage, but after a time the Emperor ordered him to be seized and publicly slain. The officer sent to arrest the Bishop, when he goes to fulfil his orders, asks him:

"Art thou Thascius Cyprian?" "I am." "Do you call yourself the father and guide of these sacrilegious Christians?" "I do." "The sacred emperor commands you to sacrifice." "I cannot." "Think what you are doing." "Perform that which is appointed you; my resolution is right, I have no need to think." After this simple, yet grand confession, and in a public square of Carthage, before a vast concourse of people, the trembling executioner, far more terrified than his victim, severed his head from his body. The man Cyprian was dead. But the wise teacher, the far-seeing leader, the spirit that could endure scorn when it was needful and meet death when that was the better, is still living and speaking, and can never die.

Cyprian was martyred in 258. Wellnigh one hundred years passed by, and in 354 A.D., Aurelius Augustine, the third and greatest of the distinguished North African teachers of the Church was born; and perhaps no theologian has had a wider influence on the thinking of the Christian world—certainly not of the Latin-speaking portion of the Church—than Augustine.

Like his predecessors he was born in North Africa, and like them, too, was a trained and accomplished rhetorician. His mother, Monnica, was a fervid, prayerful Christian, but his father seems to have been a coarse, licentious man, and the youth and early manhood of Augustine were given largely to passionate indulgence and dissipation; with all his excesses he was at the same time an omnivorous student, and soon manifested his earnestness by giving himself with sincere devotion to such of the schools of thought with which he came in contact, as appeared to promise satisfaction to his eager cravings.

The first of these was the heresy of the Manichees, the system partly Christian and partly Zoroastrian of an able Persian, Mani, from whom it took its name; this claimed to have solved the deep mystery of the origin of evil and the need of the work of Christ, by asserting the existence and activity of two equally eternal, ever contending beings, God and Satan, Good and Evil, Light and Darkness, Spirit and Matter; the good, the light, the spiritual, sought to draw all spiritual life away from the material and unite it with itself; the evil one, matter, nature, sin, holds man in the bonds of his fleshy nature and keeps him from the good; and Christ was the means by whom the release of man could alone be effected; but in himself, and in these means, the Jesus of the Manichees was wholly alien to the Christ of the Gospels.

Of course, the belief in such a system as this, false and imperfect though it was, must have won Augustine more or less from his sensual courses; but after remaining some nine years in connection with this body it failed to realize for him the lofty ideal he had sought, and he abandoned it.

About this time the writings of the new Platonists (known as the Alexandrian Philosophy), the wonderful treatises of Plotinus, and the works of Plato himself, attracted his attention. He could not study these in their original Greek, his knowledge of that language, as of the Hebrew, being very scant, but there seems to have been ample translations of them into Latin, and he refers to them continually, and in places quotes largely from their very text.

The study of the Platonists afforded him, indeed, the sublimity and philosophic depth which he had failed to find among the Manichees, and his own thought was greatly moulded in many of its most important features by his Alexandrian teachers. But much as he admired them and used their writings, they also lacked the adaptation to his spiritual needs which his soul had craved, and which his internal struggles now demanded as a necessity, if he were ever to have any true spiritual life.

While in this searching, baffled state, he came under the influence of Ambrose, the illustrious Bishop and preacher of Milan. Through the sermons and personal intercourse of this remarkable man, the interest in Christianity which had been deadened in Augustine since he left his mother's side was re-awakened, and after a considerable time of careful thought and study, he found in the Word of God, in Christ, all that he had sought so long and vainly elsewhere. About the age of thirty-three he avowed himself a Christian and was baptized. Four years later (391) he was made a Presbyter in North Africa, and four years after this, in 395, about the age of forty-one, he was chosen Assistant or Coadjutor Bishop of the diocese and city of Hippo, a considerable town on the border of the sea, about sixty miles west from Carthage and soon became, by the death of its aged Bishop, the sole Diocesan of Hippo.

In the one hundred and fifty years nearly, as it now was, since the death of Cyprian, the world had undergone one of the most stupendous revolutions in human history.

The old Roman-Greek world, with all its religions, its philosophies, its modes of life, had died. All the elements that were (twelve centuries later) to constitute modern civilization and modern Europe were in full operation, although as yet undeveloped and unrecognized in their true import.

The Emperor Constantine had struck the death-knell of the ancient world, when, in A.D. 313, he had proclaimed himself the friend and protector of the Christian Church. By summoning, in A.D. 325, the great Christian Synod or Council of Nice, and accepting its deliverances as authority, he had placed beside the Imperial throne a power that in the coming centuries would exercise a dominion wider, more imperious than any emperor of all the Cæsars' had ever dared to dream; by removing, as he did in A.D. 330, his court and capital away from old Rome, once called The Eternal City, to his new oriental seat, Constantinople, he had actually, though he knew it not, sealed the final doom of the Roman Empire in the West, and transferred the power of the Empire and the Cæsars to the barbarian Goths and the Papal hierarchy.

The history of the world from this time on is little more than on one hand the tedious, and often painful, record of the lingering decay of paganism and all the ancient life that had gathered around it, and on the other of the desolations wrought by the barbarians, and the extension of the power and influence of the Church, until it finally becomes the master of the very destroyers by whom at times its own existence had seemed to be imperilled.

In the same year (A.D. 395) in which Augustine was made Bishop, the Emperor Theodosius died, the last of the emperors who saw the Roman Empire undivided and in anything like its ancient glory. It was partitioned on his death between his two equally worthless sons, and in eighty years more the Western portion of it was wiped off the page of history, and its remains parted among the invading tribes who were rolling over it, tide after tide of destroying Goths, Vandals, Huns, Saxons, Franks, and a score of other consuming swarms from the fields and forests of the ferocious North.

With the decay of the old time religions and beliefs, which was now very universal and complete, the old virtues, and among these a spirit of manliness and bravery which belonged anciently to them, had also disappeared. With the everywhere prevailing corruption and luxury had come, as they always will, selfish, ease-seeking effeminacy, cowardice, and all the degrading, meaner vices which ever accompany an era of infidel and dissolute society.

Unhappily, too, since Christianity had become the official religion of the Emperors and the Empire, thousands had crowded into the Church without any real change of character, or any actual amendment in either their principles or life, and consequently they brought with them much of the spirit of effeminacy and self-indulgence which so disgraced the Roman paganism of that age. Hence the curious fact that the great Christian writers of this period, although expressing on the one hand their anguish at the desolations of the barbarians, yet, on the other, seem often to look upon the invaders, with all their brutality, more favorably than upon either the degenerate Roman or the false-hearted betrayers of the Christian faith. Thus a Christian writer of the times says: "We of the empire have no more victories, no more riches, no more peace; we know to increase nothing but our vices. The old Romans terrified the world, and ourselves are the terrified to-day. If we are alive at all, it is only because they think it better we should live and pay them for the wretched privilege. O, shame, shame! Who is more abject, who can be more vile than we?" Then turning in his wretchedness to the yet deeper misery of the Church defiled by its own members, he cries out: "Come, Saxons, come, Huns; come see these Christians; they read the Gospel, and live in debauchery; they listen to the apostles, and grovel in drunkenness; they claim to follow Christ, and yet are robbers."[1]

The culmination of this "Agony of the Empire" seemed to be reached when, in A.D. 410, the city of Rome itself was taken by the half-barbarous, half-heretic Alaric, and given up to his ungoverned hosts for days to sack and kill and plunder. Jerome (who noted the course of the desolation from his far-off cave in Bethlehem) had written: "The Barbarians as a deluge have devoured Egypt, Phœnicia, Syria; the whole Orient trembles; the Caucasus vomits swarms of destroying Huns, they delight in slaughter;" but when he hears of the destruction of Rome, the end of all things seems now to have come, and he cries out in his misery, "Since Rome has perished, what else can be saved?" He sees only one thing that can endure, and he believes this wholly because he believes in Christ's promise. "The Roman world has passed away, the Christians, the Christians only are left standing. It is our neck only that is not bent to the earth" in utter hopeless ruin.

It was at such a time, and amid scenes such as these, that all the later and Christian years of Augustine's life were spent. Jerome was right and Augustine felt with him, and was himself to be one

[1] Chasles, ut supra, quoting Sidonius Apollinaris, p. 103.

of the mightiest agents in aiding the Church to accomplish the tremendous work that she was now set to perform, the work of building a new world, a world of higher hopes, nobler possibilities, grander results than the history of man had ever before imagined.

To him was given a task wholly different from that of his great predecessors, Cyprian and Tertullian. Their work had been, from the conditions of their time, to contend for and to establish certain special principles or restrictions connected with the practical working of Christianity and the Church; his task was to present, in the language known to thinking men all over the Western world, and in forms adapted to their type of mind, all that was essential in the theology of the Church, and all that was proven wisest in its practical application to life and conduct.

He was, in fact, the creator of Western theology, and remains to-day, more than any other one man, the exponent of many of its chief lines of thought, the source whence all the great divisions of the Western Church, even those which seem most diverse, have drawn a large part of the principles which they deem fundamental.

This very character of his work, in connection with his wide range of subjects and his variety of treatment, will of course render it impossible to attempt here any detail of the manifold, many-sided labors of Augustine.

His chief importance in Church history, indeed in the history of the world, was that in this time of mental chaos, upheaval of ancient beliefs, annihilation of old philosophies, and the reconstruction of the world on new principles and with new aims, he presented Christianity to the Western mind in such form and under such conditions as could fill the place left vacant in men's thoughts by the obliteration of the old systems, while at the same time he announced the truths on which and by which the new order of things could be created and maintained.

Just at the period when the ancient guides of men had failed them, he gave to the thinkers of the West a coherent, elevating system of religion and of life; one which contained vital truths for the present world and rich hopes for the future life of man, and which, in its divine origin and essential truth, vastly more than compensated for the jarring uncertainties which perplexed them in the latter periods of their old pagan superstitions and half-beliefs.

He could not have known—no man could have imagined—the wonderful revolution that was to take place; but that his mind with a divine instinct felt the essential principles involved in it, is evident from the title and subject of his greatest single work, one to which he gave more than ten years of the ripest maturity of his genius and learning, " The City of God." In this he places in contrast two world powers in necessary and continual antagonism and hostility : one is the world of sin, represented by the old pagan city, heathen Rome—this he shows to be false, unsatisfying, doomed to destruction temporal and eternal; the other is the divine work and dominion of Christ, the Heavenly City, here the Church militant holding and ministering truth, warring against sin and evil, hereafter the Church triumphant and glorying with Christ forever. Hence, as the City of God it is the ever conquering, enlarging kingdom of Christ upon the earth, and the home and heaven of His elect throughout eternity.

The conception was in itself sublime and his execution of the great idea stands, and will always stand, as one, perhaps even the noblest, of the presentations of the whole scope of the Gospel which the Church in all her ages has produced.

His several personal controversies, however important they may have seemed at the time, are of comparatively small moment compared with his general influence as having given unity and completeness to the whole trend and expression of the thought of the Western Church, first directly on the times in which he lived, and then continuously, through other channels, down even to our own age with all its baffling theologies. And now, as in the former centuries, his thoughts enter as an important factor on one side or other of wellnigh every discussion on religious matters of any moment on which the minds of men are exercised.

The chief of his individual polemics were those against a schism which had revived a former contention, and which repudiated the sacraments of all ministers who were not personally holy men. It was known in the time of Augustine as Donatism, from the name Donatus, one of its African leaders. The other, which has more present interest in connection with certain lines of thought in our own time, was Pelagianism. This was originated by a monk of Britain known as Pelagius, who assigned so independent a power to the individual will of man that there was no real necessity in his salvation for any especial supernatural grace of God. God had prepared the means, and man's natural will, aided by the ordinary operations of the Divine, and working in accord with them, could do all the rest.

Augustine's own early struggles and failures had made him deeply conscious that man, of himself, was not able to elevate himself. This led him to a fierce assault on what he thought to be the unsafe and dangerous repudiation of Divine Grace by the less experienced Briton; while in another phase of his character, that profound sense of the omnipotence and supreme government of God which marked all his Christian life, constrained him to make God virtually all and in all for whatever man needed to be and to do that was right.

In both these polemics his essential principle was true and has been so recognized by the Church in all ages; but in both also his zeal, and what he thought his logic, led him to positions which have pioneered others into very lamentable errors.

From his desire to see the unity of the Church in Africa restored during the Donatist schism, he so far forgot the principles of the Gospel as he taught them elsewhere, as to urge the Emperor and civil authorities to stamp out the Donatists, who refused submission to the Church, by the hard hand of legal enactment and compulsion. Not only this, but he supports his demand, upon several occasions, by urging as a scriptural ground for it the parable of our Lord in which the servants of the Master are bidden "to go out and compel them to come in;" still more unaccountably, if possible, he urges that the example of Christ, who "cast Paul to the earth with his power," was a proof that rulers should first "compel" their unbelieving subjects to conform to the Faith and then console them with the Gospel. It needs only reference to the past history of the Church to learn what frightful evils came in after-days from the application of this unchristlike teaching in the conduct of His Church. In all fairness to so good and loving a man as Augustine surely was, we must believe that, had he known such evils would have followed from these opinions he never could have given them the sanction of his mighty name.

Another class of errors grew out of his over-strained position on the Divine omnipotence. He endeavored indeed to avoid the extremes to which his views upon this matter were liable, but in the strict logic of what he did hold, man was little more than a machine; the arbitrary sole will of God was substantially the only power, and these same principles, under the inexorable development of others who were not restrained by his large-hearted humanism, were made to conclude in the frightful doctrine "that God created a certain number of men for the express purpose of damning them;" or, in a somewhat milder form, though with no logical difference in sense, "By the decree of God, some men are predestined unto everlasting life, and others pre-ordained to everlasting death."

It may seem ungracious to refer to these mistakes or errors of so great a man, and one to whom the Church is so supremely indebted; but it is only by showing men as they really are that we can either write history correctly, or feel it can be read with profit.

When now we ask what did Augustine contribute that will help us in settling "a basis for Christian Reunion," we find that, first, he accepted as unquestionable verities all of the important principles which were presented as settled in our study of Tertullian and Cyprian. The apostolic institution of the Episcopate, the Divine authority of the Scriptures, the Diocesan independence of the Bishops, with the organic unity of the Church as a whole, and the denial of any necessity of re-baptism of those who have once been baptized with water and the formula appointed by our Lord. All these are dealt with by Augustine as matters which everyone accepts, and which are integral parts of his very conception of the Catholic Church. Besides the principles thus settled in the time of Augustine, there was another issue which has since taken a course wholly unlike that which it presented in these early ages, that is the claim of supremacy by the Bishop of Rome. The Bishop of Rome had, it is true, from time to time asserted, as we saw with Tertullian and Cyprian, that his opinions and judgments should have an especial weight and importance attached to them in certain cases by other portions of the Church. Sometimes these claims were in a general way admitted, often simply ignored, and not infrequently were in distinct terms repudiated and repelled.

This latter had been the course almost uniformly with the Church in North Africa. But a case occurred during the Episcopate of Augustine, where the issue was sharply made and the position of the African Church on its old ground, as shown by Tertullian and Cyprian, most emphatically reasserted and maintained.

In the year 418 a recalcitrant African priest, one Apiarius, being excommunicated by his Bishop, goes to Rome and seeks the favor of its Bishop Zosimus. He orders his Diocesan to restore him.[1] The Bishop

[1] Hefele's History of the Councils, English translation, vol. ii., pp. 461-481.

and Clergy of North Africa were bitterly indignant at this interference, as one of their canons prohibited any such appeal beyond the sea; the Roman Bishop sent a messenger to Carthage to repeat his demand, and he bases this demand upon the ground that it was due to him by a canon of the first and revered synod of Nice. The Africans reply that they had never heard of such Nicene canon, and that it was utterly opposed to their own law and usage; but, as the authority of the Nicene Council was supreme by the consent of all the Church, they agreed to send a deputation to Constantinople, Alexandria, and Antioch to obtain authenticated copies from the originals in these cities, in the meanwhile allowing the nominal restoration of Apiarius until the exact words of the canon of Nice should be ascertained; at the same time, they declared they would obey this if it were such as Zosimus had affirmed, but if it were not they would permit no such authority in the Bishop of Rome. After several conferences, and many angry passages, between the Roman messenger and the African Bishops, the commissioners to the East returned to Carthage and made their report, which was acted on promptly and decisively by a synod of the North African Bishops, in 424. This council declared that no such canon was to be found in any of the originals of the Synod of Nice, hence that no such authority of the Bishop of Rome had been acknowledged by that holy council; and also that the course of the Bishop of

Rome in receiving appeals from Africa was an attack[1] on the liberties of the African Church; and accordingly they begged, in respectful but very emphatic language, that he would rid them as soon as possible from the insolence of the messenger whom he had so long kept in Carthage, and would send no more men thereafter to interfere in their affairs.

The above narrative has been taken in all its essentials from the great work of the Roman Bishop Hefele on the Councils; and the only serious explanation he attempts is, that the Roman Bishop did not know what the Nicene canons really were, and had unwittingly mistaken one passed at Sardica for an act of the first and greatest of all the Christian councils. But, unfortunately, this does not help the claim of the Pope, as the power he had claimed is no more acknowledged in the Sardican canon than in any of Nice; and its value as an excuse for the Bishop of Rome is still further impaired by the fact that the successors of Zosimus, even after this crushing exposure, still continued for a considerable period to quote the Sardican canon as actually a decree of Nice.[2]

There is no doubt but Augustine attended some or all of these councils, and as he nowhere expresses any opinion inconsistent with their action, we may safely assume that he held on this matter

[1] Hefele, vol. ii., p. 480.
[2] Dictionary of Christian Biography, vol. iv., p. 1224.

the same judgment which had been pronounced by his predecessors, incorporated into the legislation of the African Church, and announced with such unmistakable clearness and vigor by the Carthaginian Council of 424, A.D.

Hence, we are entitled to conclude that the action of the North African Church as continued through all the time we know its history, and approved by all its distinguished teachers, gives no reason to regard submission to the Pope, much less a belief of his infallibility, as rightly part of any basis for the reunion of Christendom. On the contrary, all we learn from its history or hear from its great masters shows that no such claim was admitted by the African Church, but, on still stronger grounds, would have been utterly repudiated as an essential element of primitive inter-communion.

With S. Augustine ended, not only the brilliant succession of North African teachers, but virtually the North African Church and the African Provinces as distinct nationalities.

While Augustine was dying, in 430, the Vandal hordes of Genseric were besieging his city, Hippo, and ravaging to utter desolation all the country around it. The sound of the yells of the Barbarians may have mingled with the prayers and hymns which went up from his chamber of death. His eyes may have seen night after night the horizon flaming with the fires of the burning towns of his miserable people; and hardly were his funeral rites fairly over before the entire population of Hippo who had escaped death, abandoned their city a prey to the invaders, and in poverty and hopeless exile sought refuge in Italy. Carthage, too, five hundred and eighty-five years after its final conquest by Rome, became the spoil of the Northern Barbarians. And North Africa ceases henceforth to have any marked place, or play any notable part, in either the history of the old world or the work of the Church in the new.

With the death of Augustine closes in fact the period of the settlement and formulation of the fundamental principles of the Constitution, Faith, and Worship of the Church. In the ages that followed him some of these came to be perverted, some frightfully misapplied, but none that were fundamental were permanently destroyed.

In the course of centuries, the excess of a reaction against these errors and perversions has led some portions of Christendom to a neglect, and others even to a rejection, of certain of the Apostolic primitive landmarks and institutions. But there is in our day, thank God, a spirit awakening far and wide to find once more a basis whereon the dispersed sheep of Christ's flock may stand together; and may become, in the later age as in the olden time, again one fold, as we all have one Shepherd. This cannot be found in the chaotic ferment of unordered individualism; nor can it be in mediæval Romanism, or modern Papacy which has both added new doctrines to the Apostolic Faith, and subverted the primitive constitution of the Apostolic Church.

If Christendom shall ever be reunited, it must be on the basis of the creed, the orders, and the sacraments which "Holy Scriptures and ancient authors diligently read," shall evidence to have been existing "in the Church, from the Apostles' time" and through all the centuries when it yet was one.

J. F. GARRISON.

311 BENSON STREET, CAMDEN, N. J.

The School of Alexandria.

LECTURE IV.

REV. JOHN H. EGAR, D.D.,
Rector of Zion Church, Rome, N. Y.

THE SCHOOL OF ALEXANDRIA.

THERE are in this audience, I doubt not, those who have enjoyed the privilege, which has not been permitted to your lecturer, of making the voyage up the Nile. You are familiar with the present aspect of the city which bears the name of the great Greek conqueror, who founded it for the capital of his world-wide dominion. You know the unchangeable features of sea and sky, of burning sun and desert sands, of mighty river and distant hills, of pyramids almost as enduring as the mountains; and you have felt the spell of that vast and wondrous civilization of ancient Egypt, of which the ruins were around you. If, from the contemplation of the desolate temples as they are now, you can reconstruct the grandeur of those temples as they stood perfect in their glory, with their forests of pillars, their colossal statues, their avenues of sphinxes, their armies of priests, and their multitudes of worshippers, you must feel what a background they are for the scene of the conflict of Christianity with a paganism powerful enough, and earnest enough at one time, to have reared and peopled those monuments of its religion, and what a power that paganism must have still possessed at the advent of our Lord, even though its mightiest works belonged to the then distant past. And you may appreciate the visible triumph of Christianity, and the greatness of the revolution it had accomplished, when, in the year 386, the decree went forth from the Emperor Theodosius and was executed, which shut them all up, and left them to become what they are seen to be to-day.

But the Alexandria that now is, is no adequate representative of the Alexandria of the first centuries of the Christian era; nor are the ruined temples of the Nile the monuments of the life that swarmed in its busy streets. The ancient Alexandria was more a Greek than an Egyptian city; but its commercial position made it cosmopolitan. Its population of a million souls was made up of Greeks, Egyptians, and Jews, with a sprinkling of all other races. It was the centre at once of the commerce, the arts, and the learning of the time. It was, if I may so express myself, a New York for commerce, a Paris for art, for frivolity, for turbulence, and an Oxford and Cambridge for learning, all rolled into one. The outward life of Alexandria has been depicted for us in works of imagination, by two masters of the art of description[1] and no mean reputation for learning; and if their knowledge of the city is at fault, I am not able to correct it. Their historic characters, of course, have been accommodated to the needs of fiction; they have not been Zolas in picturing the vice of a heathen city; but they have represented Alexandrian life as they have conceived it from their severer studies, and we may conveniently think of it as they have drawn it. The Empire of Alexander did not last; but under the Ptolemies Alexandria grew to be of importance, and when the Roman dominion unified the three continents the advantages foreseen by its founder accrued to it. Commanding the commerce of the Nile, the Red Sea, and the Mediterranean, it became, for wealth, population, and power, the second city of the Empire. Profiting by the enlightened policy of the Ptolemies, who desired to know the world opened to them by the Macedonian conquests, it became the centre of learning. Its great library was one of the wonders of the world; and though the core of its culture was Greek, it interested itself in all other intellectual developments, and the theosophies of the East, the traditional lore of the Egyptians, the sacred scriptures of the Jews, were welcome subjects for its inquiring minds, as well as the poetry and philosophy of the Greeks, and the physical science of the age. The cultivated

[1] Charles Kingsley in Hypatia, and George Ebers in several works.

Alexandrian was above all things cosmopolitan. He aimed to know everything, to be everything, to harmonize everything. His chief deity was none of the traditional deities of the Egyptians, or Greeks, or Romans, or Syrians; it was Serapis, an importation from the shores of the Black Sea, whose previous obscurity permitted him to be invested with such attributes as the Alexandrian mind conceived to belong to Deity in general, and under whom, or beside whom, could coexist all the other deities which any idolator had been brought up to worship.

Into this great, wealthy, luxurious, learned, proud city, at some time in the second half of the first century, entered the Evangelist St. Mark with a few companions, to convert it to the Christian faith. What were the means and conditions of success? Conceive a Christian congregation once established, what were the arms with which it was to contend against all that array of worldliness? The answer is very simple, but implies a great deal. S. Mark came with *the Gospel in the Church.* The Christian congregation once established in Alexandria, proclaimed the Gospel in the Church. That, I say, is the answer; but it implies a great deal. For what is the Gospel in the Church?

Before we proceed to answer this question, let us look at some of the providential provisions, in the age preceding our Lord, for opening the way for the Gospel in this city of Alexandria. M. Guizot somewhere has the remark that Christianity was planted at the confluence of *three* great civilizations, the Hebrew, the Greek, and the Roman. I venture the emendation that Christianity was planted at the confluence of *four* great civilizations, the Hebrew, the Greek, the Roman, and the Oriental. For, surely we must not overlook the power and influence of that great Oriental civilization which had been developed in Egypt, Assyria, and Babylon; nor may we think it was sufficiently represented by the Hebrew. We cannot understand the early history of Christianity and its conflicts with heresy, unless we allow for the influence of Orientalism in the Gnostic sects. Now, Alexandria was the meeting-place of all these civilizations; it was that which gave it its cosmopolitan character. Especially were the Jews numerous and influential there. The policy of Alexander and the earlier Ptolemies gave them equal political privileges with the Macedonians; and as a great part of the commerce and banking of the city was in their hands, they associated on equal terms with the other races in Alexandria, and learned to accommodate themselves to their surroundings. Now, it is one law of the Providential training of mankind, that position influences thought. The thought of the individual, whoever he may be, has relation to his age, his country, and his circumstances. The Jew in Alexandria being in a different position to that of the Jew in Palestine—being in contact with the great world of commerce, of movement, of thought—could not be exclusive like the Palestinian Rabbi. He was put where he was by Divine Providence to see another side of Divine Revelation—to see its relations to the world at large—relations which the Rabbi at Jerusalem, with his Pharisaic exclusiveness, could not see. Among other things, he gave up the Hebrew language and became a Hellenist, that is, a Greek-speaker. It was for the Jews of Alexandria that the Septuagint version of the Old Testament was made—the first example, it is said, of the translation of a book from one language into another; and so it came to pass that the sacred scriptures of the Mosaic covenant were accessible, not only to the Jews of the dispersion, but to such of the Gentile world as might desire to investigate them. But the learned Jews of Alexandria not only translated their scriptures into Greek; they studied the Greek philosophers; and so there arose the Hellenistic School, the exponent of a wider and more catholic Old Testament theology than that of the Rabbis of Palestine; one that found points of contact between the Hebrew prophets and the sages of Greece. You remember how Apollos is spoken of in the Acts of the Apostles, as "an eloquent man and mighty in the Scriptures." He was a learned Alexandrian, the representative in Scripture of that school, which was an important intermediary between Gentile culture and Hebrew orthodoxy.

The most illustrious member of the Jewish

school of Alexandria was Philo. He was a young man at the birth of our Lord, and lived till the middle of the first century. Though there is no evidence that Philo became a Christian, the influence of his writings must have been great upon the Christian thinkers of Alexandria, as it was upon the philosophers of the succeeding age. In fact, the influence of this Jew upon Alexandrian philosophy is one of the most remarkable phenomena of the period. At the time of Philo, Greek philosophy was virtually dead. It had asked all possible questions, and failing to find an answer, it had degenerated in the New Academy into general skepticism and empty disputation. Philo regenerated it by giving it a new principle and a new doctrine. He had been trained in the knowledge of the Old Testament scriptures: he had come to see in them, by his method of allegorical interpretation, a hidden mystery in every word; and so he brought to Greek philosophy the new principle of Faith—not as rational belief upon evidence divinely attested, but as the intuition of things divine; and the new doctrine of the *Logos*, or Divine Word, not as S. John reveals Him, the eternal Son of the Father, but as the chief of a world of " Potencies," or Powers, the revealers and agents of the absolute, incomprehensible Deity. It is not to be admitted that Alexandrian theology is to be traced back to Philo rather than to S. John, or that S. John borrowed from Philo; the difference between Philo and S. John has been well said to be that the Logos of Philo is a medium of disjunction, separating God from the world; the Logos of the New Testament one of conjunction; in Philo it is because God is so far, in the New Testament because He is so near; in Philo the Logos is an unreal, in the New Testament a real and essential Personality. While, then, Philo was studied by the Alexandrian Fathers as an expositor of the Old Testament, and influenced them not altogether well by his excessive allegorism, they had in S. John's Gospel the corrective of his error, and were in no need of learning their theology from him. But in the domain of philosophy, where there was not this safeguard, his influence was immense. His doctrine of the Logos and other Potencies was the starting-point of the Alexandrian Gnostic systems; and after they had run their course it was the inspiration of the Neo-Platonic School, which was for centuries the shadow and the antagonist of Christianity. So that Philo was an authority in widely-differing and opposed schools. I say Philo, but Philo as the representative of the Hellenistic School of Alexandria. And so it was that in this way the higher questions involved in Christianity became of interest to the thinkers of Alexandria, and so the Hellenistic School was an element in the preparation for Christianity in that city; because, when questions are once started, people are at least willing to hear those who profess to be able to answer them.

Let us now return to our question—what were the arms with which the first preachers in Alexandria were furnished to subdue it to Christianity?

S. Mark and his associates did not come to the great city to teach the philosophy of Philo or any other philosophy; they came to *bear witness to the facts* of the life, death, and resurrection of our Lord Jesus Christ, and to press home upon the conscience the need of salvation through Him. Their preaching was the assertion of those facts which are witnessed to in the records of the four Evangelists, one of whom was S. Mark himself, and which are summed up once for all in the Apostles' and Nicene Creeds. Put yourselves in the presence of polytheism, of a philosophy which justifies polytheism, of an eclectic philosophy which includes all polytheisms, and you will see that these truths of the Apostles' and Nicene Creeds are no arbitrarily selected propositions, but the fundamental truths which it is necessary to insist upon, in order to turn the hearer from polytheism, from error, from idolatry, to the worship of the one true God, and to salvation through our Lord Jesus Christ. Perhaps in saying this I am only repeating what has been said in other lectures of this course. If so, I beg that you will pardon the iteration, for it is necessary to my subject. The Creed is simply the Gospel, so to speak, in portable form. The Creed is the Gospel, and the Gospel is the Creed; the contents of each are equal; they are the same. The facts confessed in the Creed were the facts taught by S. Mark and his successors in the first period of the Alexandrian Church, as in every period of its history. That was the foundation. That is the faith once delivered to the saints. That was the basis of the Alexandrian theology, as of all Catholic theology whatsoever.

But further:—The convert to this Creed was, by the fact of believing it—not merely as an orthodox confession, but as a living faith—called and pledged to a life of purity, of honesty, of charity, of devotion, of holiness. His faith wrought repentance and amendment of life, hatred of sin and love of God, separation from the wickedness of the world, communion with God, and association with the people of God. It imposed upon him, therefore, for reasons natural, and for reasons supernatural—for discipline, for safeguard, for training and instruction, for special helps of Divine grace, for the means of advancement in holiness—the obligation of becoming incorporate, through the sacrament of baptism, in the visible Church, the community of the professed followers of Jesus Christ; and of preserving his organic union with that body and with its Head, through the Sacrament of the Holy Communion.

Again:—By this admission to and continuance in the communion of the Church, he was placed under the supervision and government of its appointed and lawfully ordained officers, the bishops and clergy, and united in the bond of brotherhood with all its members, wheresoever dispersed throughout the world, and especially in his own locality. Moreover, if he were unfaithful, and therefore excluded from the communion of the Church, he was felt to be no longer in a state of salvation. No one can read the early records of Christianity without finding that the Church took this ground with regard to its members from the very first; and you will see, if you reflect a moment, that it could not do otherwise. At the present day, when Christianity is brought face to face with heathenism in the mission field, it is obliged to take the same ground. The missionary, whatever be his denominational standard, must and does act upon the method of the early Church, because it is the only method of dealing with the circumstances.

This, then, is the foundation never to be lost sight of in tracing the course of Alexandrian theological thought. Let me here, then, call your attention to one of the lessons we are to learn from these lectures. Manifestly, in appealing to the thinking mind of a philosophic and cosmopolitan people, the first need is to get them to have a real grasp of the facts, that is, a real faith in them. The very atmosphere of toleration in which such a people lives is apt to generate an easy indifference or careless acquiescence, instead of a real faith; and to create in the mind of the thinker who cares to consider them, the disposition to explain them away so as to make them fit into his own eclectic system. I ask you to take notice, then, how Christianity from the very beginning adopted the method of the inductive philosophy—of that philosophy which dominates us at the present day—of that philosophy of which Bacon is the expounder, and which we recognize as the mother of all true science —the method which starts with facts, and upon the solid basis of facts erects its edifice of reasoning. The principle is that *facts are superior to theories;* and it was by maintaining this principle that the faith of the Church overcame all the philosophies of the ancient world. Facts are superior to theories, and therefore, when the fact and the theory come in conflict, the theory must give way to the fact, and not the fact to the theory. So it was that Christianity entered in among the philosophical theories of the ancient world, and among the philosophical theories of that great and learned city of Alexandria. It proclaimed certain facts of which it had sufficient witness. "That which was from the beginning," says S. John in his first Epistle, "which we have heard, which we have seen with our eyes, which we have looked upon and our hands have handled of the Word of life . . . . that which we have seen and heard, declare we unto you." "We are witnesses of these things," say the Apostles in the Acts, time and again; and so it was everywhere. Now, these facts of the life and death and resurrection of our blessed Lord, of which the Apostles were witnesses, of which the Apostolic office is the continuous witness to the end of the world, will not fit into any false philosophy, whether it be the dualism or pantheism of the first, or the materialism of the nineteenth century. And therefore the first question, in the first or the nineteenth century, upon which it depends whether the answerer is a Christian at all or not, is, Do you accept the facts? or, as the baptismal interrogatory is, " Dost thou believe all the articles of the Christian faith as contained in the Apostles' Creed?" If you do, then, your philosophy being true and right, will find here its explanation and completion; but if it be a false and wrong philosophy, it will find here its correction and antidote. That was how Christianity entered into the thought of the world, not in Alexandria only, but everywhere. That was how it fought its fight and won its victories. That was the line which divided the theology of the Church from the speculations of the heretics. The heretic pared away the facts of the faith to fit his theories; the Catholic theologian fitted his theories to his facts, he built up his theology on the faith once delivered to the saints. The truths or facts, divinely revealed if supernatural, sensibly perceived if natural—the truths or facts of the unity of God, of the Eternal Sonship, of the Incarnation of the Son of God, of His human life, death, and resurrection, of the Holy Spirit, of the Catholic Church as a visible and really existing society, of the forgiveness of sins, the future resurrection, and the life everlasting—these were preached as facts, not as speculations, or opinions, or theories; they were to dominate theories because they are facts, and only as they are accepted for facts is a Christian theology possible. That was true in the first century, it is just as true in the nineteenth.

The difference, then, between the theologians of the Alexandrian Church and the heretical teachers who claimed after a sort the Christian name, was that the theologians followed what Clement and Origen call "the ecclesiastical rule;" while the heretics interpreted or mutilated Holy Scripture and the Christian faith according to notions and opinions current in the outside world. Now, the first evidence we have of literary or intellectual activity in the Alexandrian Church comes to us in connection with the appearance of heretical teachers; and this explains what is perhaps the earliest contemporary notice of that Church now extant—a notice which, unless this circumstance is attended to, would convey a very unfavorable impression. For half or three-quarters of a century after its foundation, the Church in Alexandria pursued the even tenor of its way, leaving few or no written memorials to attest its works of faith, of piety, and charity. And yet by the reign of Hadrian (A.D. 117-138) it had become so important that that versatile, superficial, and inquisitive Emperor, in a letter to his friend, the Consul Servianus, thus describes the state of public opinion as he found it in Alexandria: "I have become," he says, "perfectly familiar with Egypt, which you praised to me. It is fickle, uncertain, blown about by every gust of rumor. Those who worship Serapis are Christians, and those are devoted to Serapis who call themselves bishops of Christ. There is no ruler of a synagogue there, no Samaritan, no Christian presbyter, who is not an astrologer, a sooth-sayer, a quack. The patriarch himself [*i.e.*, the Jewish patriarch, for there were no Christian patriarchs at this time], whenever he comes to Egypt, is compelled by some to worship Serapis, by others to worship Christ." Now, it is safe to say that, as a notice of the real Church in Alexandria, this is not true or near the truth, and that Hadrian had little or no acquaintance with that Church. As a satirical comment upon the state of public opinion, and a witness to the syncretistic spirit which lay at the foundation of the Gnostic heresies of Alexandria, it has its value. But it shows incidentally how great had been the progress of the Church, even at this early period, thus to infuse into the whole atmosphere of the city an interest in Christianity. This letter of Hadrian is illustrated by one or two quotations from Clement and Origen, which I wish to read to you. Clement is prosecuting the argument that the true doctrine is that which has been preserved in the Church from the beginning, and that the " human assemblies" which the heretics called together were posterior to the Catholic Church. " For the teaching of our Lord at His advent," he says, " beginning with Augustus and Tiberius, was completed in the middle of the time of Tiberius. And that of the Apostles, including the ministry of Paul, ends with Nero. It was later, in the times of Hadrian the King, that those who invented the heresies arose; and they continued to the times of Antoninus."[1] Now, Origen makes the acute remark "that heresies of different kinds have never originated from any matter in which the principle involved was not important and beneficial to human life." He is answering the objection of Celsus, that Christianity is unworthy of attention because "the Christians were divided and split up into factions, each individual desiring to have his own party." Origen replies with the remark just quoted, that Christianity is for that very reason worth attending to, because heresies do not arise in a matter of no interest or importance. He instances the various schools of medicine and philosophy, and proceeds: "So, then, seeing Christianity appeared an object of veneration, not to the servile class only, as Celsus supposes, but to many among the Greeks who were devoted to literary pursuits, there necessarily originated heresies, not as the result of faction and strife, but through the earnest desire of many literary men to become acquainted with the doctrines of Christianity."[2] This was natural in an age of inquiry, and in an eclectic city like Alexandria, where knowledge was encyclopædic in its range, and endeavored to in-

[1] Stromata VII., 17. [2] Origen against Celsus, III., 13.

clude all opinions. It explains, as I said, Hadrian's satire, not upon Christianity, but upon Alexandria. If you reflect, you will see that just such "literary men" were the ones who were likely to fall into Hadrian's way, and from whom he would form his opinion of the Alexandrians. But you will see also that Christianity must have made great progress in Alexandria, to have impressed so many literary men with a desire to appropriate from it in making up their systems, just as soon as tolerant emperors, as Trajan and Hadrian were, began to discourage wholesale persecution.

The heretics of this period are those known as Gnostics. They have been brought before you in the Lecture on the School of Antioch; and I shall only remark that, while the philosophical basis of the Syrian Gnosticism was dualism, that of the Alexandrian was pantheism; and that under this guiding principle the Alexandrian Gnostic endeavored to form, in accordance with the genius of the city, a comprehensive system which would explain and justify all the various religions and philosophies of the ancient world, and combine them in a harmonious whole. Now, no one could do that with Christianity, without finding it necessary to falsify the record, to explain away the facts, to say in effect: We understand this better than the writers of the Gospel, and the teachers of the Church; we are able to penetrate below the surface; we have insight to see the truth underlying their statements; we can correct their mistakes. That is why these speculators are called heretics, rather than philosophers. A philosopher who simply left Christianity out of his system was not a heretic, he was a heathen; a philosopher who took a mutilated or falsified version of the facts of the Gospel into his system was a heretic, because he depraved the faith.

It would be a great mistake to think that the Gnostic heresiarchs were not profound thinkers, or earnest men; and yet it is true, as Professor Salmon says, that "the zeal with which a learner commences the study of ecclesiastical history is not infrequently damped at an early stage, when he finds that, in order to know the history of religious thought in the second century, he must make himself acquainted with speculations so wild and so baseless that it is irksome to read them, and difficult to believe that time was, when acquaintance with them was counted as what alone deserved the name of 'knowledge.'" The conclusion which he draws from this is valuable for some among us at the present day. "Every union of philosophy and religion is the marriage of a mortal with an immortal; the religion lives; the philosophy grows old and dies. When the philosophic element of a theological system becomes antiquated, its explanations, which contented one age, become unsatisfactory to the next, and there ensues what is spoken of as a conflict between religion and science; whereas it is in reality a conflict between the science of one generation and that of a preceding one." Reflection upon this truth is much to be commended to some of our philosophic theologians. So long as theology is true to its own tradition as realized in the Catholic creeds, it is like the Lord Jesus Christ, of whom it witnesses, "the same yesterday, and to-day, and forever." Certainly this is the lesson taught by the mistakes, not only of the Gnostic heretics of Alexandria, but of the great philosophic theologian of its Catholic School, the saintly but unsainted Origen.

We cannot understand Clement of Alexandria, without some knowledge of Basilides and Valentinus, the heads of two opposite schools of Alexandrian Gnostics. The moral principles of Basilides were ascetic, those of Valentinus antinomian. I shall not attempt to explain their systems, but shall content myself with a single observation upon each. The aim of all the Gnostic systems was, like that of Philo, to bridge over the distance between the absolute, unconditioned, infinite God, and the finite and conditioned universe. Basilides held the supreme Being to be so absolute and so unconditioned that he could not predicate anything whatsoever of him, not even existence—he could not say even that *He is*. If therefore you reduce the account of his theology and cosmology given in Hippolytus[1] to its simplest terms, it may be stated thus: That the primeval *Nothing* at first produced *Something*, and that from that Something grew *Everything*.

[1] Hippolytus: Refutation of all Heresies, VII., 9 sq.

"There is nothing new under the sun," and it would be difficult to find a more complete, condensed, and comprehensive statement of the modern doctrine of evolution than this. The system of Valentinus was the extreme illustration of the position "whatever is, is right;" and for that reason moral progress was impossible under it. Perverting S. Paul, Valentinus held that mankind were of three different natures, and that their conduct was the result of their organization, and therefore involved no moral responsibility. You remember that S. Paul, at the close of the First Epistle to the Thessalonians, says: "I pray God your whole spirit and soul and body be preserved blameless;" and that in different places he speaks of the "carnal" man, the "natural"—or, to turn the Greek word into English, the "psychical" man, and the "spiritual" man. Valentinus therefore thought that some men were wholly material or carnal in nature; these were heathens worshipping material deities or idols, because they could not be anything else; they were sensualists in morals, because they had no higher moral power. Other men had a body and soul; these were the "natural" or "psychical" men of S. Paul; they were Jews and ordinary Christians; they worshipped the Creator and observed his law, which was contained in the Old Testament, and after this life would go to a soul-heaven. But then, this Creator whom they worshipped was not the Supreme God; there was above him a spiritual God, and a spiritual heaven, reserved for the spiritual men, that is, the Gnostics, who being "spiritual," were not under the law, being made perfect by knowledge.

You will ask how such a doctrine could be counted sufficiently Christian to be called heretical. And yet, if you had the original documents you would be astonished to find how much Scripture they could pervert to favor their dogmas; and you would see the value of the faith of the Church as the interpreter of Scripture. The Valentinians were heretics because they depraved the faith in Christ to accommodate it to these ideas. According to them, Jesus or Saviour was one person, Christ was another. Jesus was a spiritual emanation from the region of the Supreme; Christ was a psychical creature from the region of the Creator. Christ lived upon earth thirty years in the practice of virtue according to the law, and then at his baptism, Jesus or Saviour came down upon him, and he became Jesus Christ. As this twofold being, it was his mission to enlighten the "spiritual" men with the true *gnosis* which made them Gnostics, and so to prepare them for the spiritual heaven. Having accomplished this by his teachings, the Saviour forsook Christ, and Christ alone then wrought the redemption for "psychic" natures by suffering upon the cross. As there is no redemption for material or "carnal" natures, they simply perish, and the material world will be annihilated in the fire which shall be at the last day.

If you have condescended to follow me thus far, you see some of the problems which were to be solved by the Catholic theologians of the School of Alexandria. They were, first of all, to uphold the teaching of the Church, the integrity of the Gospel, and the truths and facts of the faith as handed down from the beginning. They were to present to the thinkers of the great city a theology of the Creed and the Scriptures which should not only refute Gnosticism and heathen philosophy, but which should draw to itself the philosophic mind by true explanations of the relation of the Creator to the creation, and of the Saviour to the souls He came to save. They must present also a philosophy of human life and conduct which should show every man to be saveable, which should invite every man to faith, and which should lead the disciple onward to that true *gnosis* which is the knowledge of God, and of His Son, Jesus Christ, our Lord. They must, in a word, not only release philosophy from Gnostic speculations, but lead it captive to the obedience of Christ.

In Clement and Origen, the Alexandrian Church found teachers competent for the work before them. They were successively heads of the Catechetical School of Alexandria, which under them became a renowned centre of Christian learning. I want you to understand what this Catechetical School was, as its peculiar character has much to do with our properly understanding Clement. It was not a theological seminary, as we understand the term. It was not a school for training clergy in the knowledge, theoretical or practical, appertaining to their profession. It was primarily the school for the Catechumens—that is, for those who were investigating or being instructed in Christian doctrine preparatory to their baptism. Originally it was not a school for the members of the Church at all, but for those who were seeking admission to the Church. It was a school after the manner of the philosophical schools which were so numerous in Alexandria—a school, not for boys, but for grown-up men and women, held in the house of the teacher, and free to all who chose to attend. As Christianity attracted the attention of the educated class, men who were graduates of other schools, or even masters in them, might be scholars in this. It was imperative, therefore, that the teacher be a man of intellect and learning, well versed in the science and philosophy of the age, and able to cope with the bright minds among his hearers. Such men were Pantænus, Clement, and Origen. They gave the Catechetical School a high intellectual character, discussed philosophy in its relation to Christianity, and solved the difficulties and confirmed the faith of the cultured catechumen. The curriculum in certain directions was perhaps in advance of what that of a professional school intended exclusively for the clergy would have been. I say in certain directions; but there was one limitation imposed upon it, by its nature as a Catechetical School, which must be taken into account in studying the works that emanated from it. The times of which I am speaking were times when the Christians were exposed to persecution, and therefore when it was necessary for the Church to guard its assemblies from intrusion, and its mysteries from profanation. It was therefore, of necessity, organized in some sort as a secret society whose pass-words, as the Lord's Prayer and the Creed, whose sacraments and peculiar usages, and the doctrines of grace they implied, were not formally explained or taught to the believer until his constancy had been tested, and he had been actually initiated by baptism. In the Catechetical School, therefore, it being a school for the uninitiated, these matters were carefully and enigmatically alluded to, in language which would be understood only by those who were in full communion with the Church. This, it seems to me, is what is meant by the *disciplina arcani*, or "discipline of the secret," of which we read in this period of Church history.

Now, it is from not attending to this that a wrong impression prevails concerning the teachings of Clement of Alexandria. It is supposed by some that he deals with the subjects before him as a philosophic theologian, with no Church tradition behind him; whereas he really deals with them as a Catechist, and as an author whose writings were intended for those who were not of the Church, as well as for those who were. In the first chapter of the *Stromata* Clement declares his method. His instructors, he says, preserving the tradition of the blessed doctrine from the holy Apostles Peter and James, and John and Paul, transmitted it to him. He stores up his memoranda, therefore, as an outline of the vigorous discourses he was privileged to hear, and as a memorial of blessed and remarkable men. But in doing so he observes a wise caution. " The mysteries," he says, " are delivered mystically, that what is spoken may be in the mouth of the speaker ; rather not in his voice, but in his meaning." " Some things I purposely omit in the exercise of a wise selection, . . . some things my treatise will hint ; on some it will linger ; some it will merely mention. . . . The dogmas taught by remarkable sects will be adduced, and to these will be opposed what ought to be said. . . so that we may have our ears ready for the reception of the tradition of true knowledge, the soil being cleared of thorns and weeds in order to the planting of the true vine."

And so it is that, as the very last thing in the extant portion of the *Stromata* (for it is incomplete, and was never finished), Clement shows that all his labor has been to lead the thinking reader to the Church. Immediately following the passage which I quoted concerning the antiquity of the Church doctrine and the lateness of the heresies, Clement says : " The true Church, that which is really ancient, is *one*, and in it are enrolled those who, according to

God's purpose, are just. For because God is one, and the Lord one, that which is most honorable is lauded for its singleness, being an imitation of the One. In the nature of the One, then, is associated in joint heritage the One Church, which the heretics strive to cut asunder into many sects. . . . The pre-eminence of the Church, as the principle of union, is in its oneness, in this surpassing all things else, and having nothing like or equal to itself."

This is from that which is almost the concluding paragraph of Clement's great work—his Trilogy, I might call it, for it includes three separate yet connected treatises from which his teaching is to be gathered. They are, The Exhortation to the Greeks; the Instructor, so-called; and the *Stromateis*, a word meaning patchwork, and translated "Miscellanies," because of its discursive character. Their object is, I must insist, not to present the theology of the Church in its completeness, but rather to serve as an introduction to theology proper—to carry on Clement's work as a Catechist by withdrawing the reflecting mind outside the Church from the false *gnosis* of the heretics, and bringing it to seek the true *gnosis* of the Christian life. They show a man of immense reading, and could have been written nowhere but in the vicinity of a great library like that of Alexandria.

In the Exhortation to the Greeks, Clement pleads with them to abandon the impious mysteries of idolatry for the adoration of the Divine Word and the Father; he exposes the absurdity of their myths, their sacrifices, and their images; he shows that by Divine help, some of their philosophers and poets caught glimpses of the truth; he answers the objection that it is not right to abandon the customs of their fathers; and shows how great are the benefits conferred on man through the coming of Christ. His object in this book is to invite to faith and baptism, and the way in which he speaks of baptism in this treatise may illustrate what I have said of his method of allusion to the Sacraments. In the chapter on forsaking the customs of their fathers, he says: "Receive then the water of the Word; wash, ye polluted ones; purify yourself from custom by sprinkling yourselves with the drops of truth." In what way, he asks in another place, is a stranger permitted to enter the Kingdom of Heaven? and answers, "When he is enrolled and made a citizen, and receives one to stand to him in the relation of father [he alludes, you see, to the sponsor or godfather at baptism]; then he will be occupied with the Father's concerns; then shall he be deemed worthy to be made his heir; then will he share the Kingdom of the Father with his own dear Son. For this is the Church of the First-born, composed of many good children; these are the first-born enrolled in heaven, who hold high festival with so many myriads of angels." Again he veils his meaning by an allusion to the heathen mysteries while speaking of the Church: "O truly sacred mysteries! O stainless light! My way is lighted with torches and I survey the heavens and God; I become holy while I am initiated. The Lord is the hierophant, and seals while illuminating him who is initiated, and presents to the Father him who believes, to be kept safe forever. . . . If it is thy wish, be thou also initiated, and thou shalt join the choir of angels around the unbegotten and indestructible and only true God, the Word of God raising the hymn with us. This Jesus, who is eternal, the one great High Priest of the one true God and His Father, prays for and exhorts men."

In the last two sentences we may perceive an allusion to the Eucharistic service, to the *Trisagion* Hymn, and to the Consecration Prayer, but so as not to reveal the mysteries to the uninitiated. The members of the Church would understand; the others would not—and that was Clement's intention. In the same veiled way he speaks in a passage in the *Stromata*, when his meaning is plain to those who can read between the lines: "'Taste and see that the Lord is Christ,' it is said. For so He imparts of Himself to those who partake of such food in a more spiritual manner; where the soul nourishes itself, according to the truth-loving Plato. For the knowledge of the Divine essence is the meat and drink of the Divine Word. Wherefore, also, Plato says in the second book of the Republic:— 'It is those who sacrifice, not some cheap thing,'[1]

[1] Literally "a pig."

but some great and difficult sacrifice,' who ought to inquire respecting God. And the Apostle writes, 'Christ our Passover is sacrificed for us'—a sacrifice indeed hard to procure, even the Son of God consecrated for us."[1]

So again he speaks of the ministry of the Church in the same allusive way, as in the following passage, where he is speaking of degrees of glory in heaven, and saying that those who attain the highest holiness shall have the chief seats in the heavenly Kingdom. "Those, then, who have exercised themselves in the Lord's commandments and lived perfectly according to the gospel, may be enrolled [hereafter] in the chosen body of the Apostles. Such an one is in reality a presbyter of the Church, and a true deacon of the will of God, if he do and teach what is the Lord's; not as being ordained by men, nor regarded righteous because a presbyter, but enrolled in the presbyterate because righteous. And although here on earth he be not honored with the chief seat [*i.e.*, the seat of the bishop], he will [there] sit down on the four and twenty thrones, judging the people as John says in the Apocalypse. . . . For, according to my opinion, the grades here in the Church of bishops, presbyters, deacons, are imitations of the angelic glory, and of that economy which the Scriptures say awaits those who, following the footsteps of the Apostles, have lived in perfection of righteousness according to the Gospel."[2]

[1] Stromata, V., 10.   [2] Ib., VI., 13.

You see clearly from these extracts what Clement's method was in dealing, in these works, with those matters of Church polity and sacramental grace which, in an age of contradiction and persecution, were not for prudential reasons spoken of openly to the outside world; and you see also that, so understood, his testimony is the same as that of the other Fathers, to the ministry and worship of the Church. To return to our analysis of his writings: The second work, "The Instructor," is practical. The English word used for the title of the translation does not accurately express the Greek. Clement calls it the παιδαγωγος, from which we have the two words *page* and *pedagogue*. The Greek παιδαγωγος was not the schoolmaster or instructor; but the attendant, governor, or page who led the young child to the schoolmaster, and who had the supervision, not of his education, but of his conduct and manners. In this book, then, Clement represents Christ as the "Page" of the Christian after baptism, forming his manners according to the Gospel. His object in this treatise is to speak to the outside world, as well as to the children of the Church; and so, observing the same reserve as before, he deals with the external behavior of Christians in their intercourse with the world. It is in fact a treatise upon manners and morals, rather than on ethics; and it leads to the ethical science of the *Stromata*. "Our superintendence in instruction and discipline," he says, "is the object of the Word, from whom we learn frugality, humility, and all that pertains to love of truth, love of man, and love of excellence. In the case of those who are trained by this influence, even their gait in walking, their sitting at table, their food, their sleep, their going to bed, their regimen, and their mode of life, acquire a superior dignity. Not only is it requisite to contemplate the Divine, we must also contemplate human nature, to live as the truth directs, and to admire the instructor and his injunctions; according to whose image, conforming ourselves to Him, and making the word and our deeds agree, we ought to live a real life."

Having thus shown the outside world how Christianity forms the manners and earthly life of the Christian, Clement proceeds in the *Stromata* to show how it makes him a true Gnostic. To the mere reader the *Stromata* must be very tiresome, while to the student it is the most interesting of Clement's works. It seems to me that he had a threefold object in writing it: the first was to allure the higher intellect of the Greeks to Christianity; the second, to lay down a true philosophy of human nature, in opposition to the speculations of Basilides, Valentinus, and other false Gnostics; and the third, to stimulate the Christian disciple to a wider culture and a sympathetic interest in the intellectual world around him. It is evident, from the way in which the *Stromata* begins, that it was a question with some whether he ought to write at all; and he has several times to allude to the narrowness of certain among the brethren.

This explains Clement's attitude with regard to philosophy. He knew very well that persons are brought together by understanding one another; and therefore it was for his interest as a catechist, as well as from his conviction as a scholar, that he asserted philosophy to be a divine gift to the Greeks, and a preparation of the Gentile world for Christianity. Clement did not do what Origen did to his hurt, accept philosophy as supplementary to revelation and the tradition of the Church; he did not compound a doctrine partly philosophical and partly religious; what he did was to show that Christianity had the criterion by which to judge of philosophy, and the means of bringing it to perfection; and therefore that the philosopher, having been brought so far on his way by philosophy, needed Christianity for his completion. "At one time," he says, "philosophy justified the Greeks—not conducting them to perfect righteousness, but as the first and second flights of steps help you in your ascent to the upper room, and as the grammarian helps the philosopher. But the teaching which is in Christ is complete in itself and without defect, being the 'power and wisdom of God,' and the Hellenic philosophy does not by its approach make the truth more powerful." And here a remark is necessary as to Clement's idea of philosophy. "By philosophy," he says, "I do not mean the

Stoic, or the Platonic, or the Epicurean, or the Aristotelian; but whatever has been well said by any of those sects which teach righteousness along with a science pervaded by piety—this eclectic whole I call philosophy."[1] Now, it has been well said that in the region of pure philosophy an eclectic system is an impossibility. For how is one to choose out from the various systems that which is fit and right and true, unless one has beforehand a criterion of truth, that is, a system of his own? But the previous system, according to which one is to judge and to select, is the real philosophy, and its preexistence negatives eclecticism. In the region of pure philosophy this is a valid objection; but it does not touch Clement, because in the Christian faith he had a criterion of judgment, and in the ecclesiastical rule and tradition of which he has so much to say, and the importance of which I pointed out at the beginning of this lecture.

The position, which is undoubtedly a true one, that philosophy was a gift to the Greeks from the Divine Word, the Eternal Son, who became flesh and dwelt among us; who, as He gave the Law and the Prophets to the Jews, left Himself not without witness among the nations of the earth, was of immense use to Clement in that it furnished the basis for the complete refutation of the Gnostic heresies of all kinds. For if the Divine Logos had thus secretly prompted the Greeks to search for truth

[1] Stromata, I., 7.

and to prepare for His coming, it was because they and all mankind, as well as all things visible and invisible, were the creatures, not of a subordinate Creator, but of the infinite and supreme Father, by the Son, through the Holy Spirit. And so the whole Gnostic Pleroma, with its Eons, its Demiurge, and its distinction of spiritual and psychic heavens, was swept away at once. So surely does the statement of the truth bring to nought the ignorance of foolish men. It vindicated also the unity of human nature, and the spiritual capacity of all men for the truth as revealed in Christ. Men are not of different natures, some material, some psychic, and some spiritual. The carnal or natural man, in S. Paul's phrase, is the man who rejects the spiritual wisdom of the Word; the spiritual man is he who follows it. So it put upon its true ground the distinction between faith and knowledge, and their mutual dependence. The Gnostics held that sense was the material intellect; that faith was the relation between the psychic soul and the Demiurge, or finite creator; and that knowledge was the spiritual illumination of the Gnostic, lifting him up to the absolute and unconditioned Supreme Being. Clement spends much time in demonstrating that faith is not the attribute of a particular nature, but an act of the soul reaching out to God and accepting the revelation of Christ; that knowledge is not the attribute of another nature, but that it is the passing of faith into certainty; and therefore, that faith is the foundation of all true knowledge. So again, matter is not evil, and the body is not evil; and therefore, the true Gnostic does not despise the body, but keeps it in subjection; he neither practises a degrading asceticism, nor indulges in corrupt living; he is willing to be a martyr for the truth, but is not needlessly to expose himself; he lives in that communion with God which makes him content, whether present in the body, or absent with the Lord.

The work of Clement against the false Gnosticism was successful. From his time it declined in importance, and its place in opposition to Christianity was taken by Neo-Platonism. My time does not permit any examination of the Neo-Platonic system, and I shall make but one observation upon it. The need that the soul feels of times of conscious communion with God, closer than that sense of constant dependence on Divine Providence which is the habit of the believing mind, is realized in the Church in prayer, in worship, and in the Holy Communion. Over against this, in all the non-Christian or uncatholic systems which have felt the need, there has been the attempt to realize it in the state of ecstasy or enthusiasm—using the word in the philosophical sense. This was the great practical opposition between Neo-Platonism and Christianity. In the approach to God through Christ, Christianity is sacramental; in the approach to its philosophical deity, Neo-Platonism was extatic, enthusiastic, and theurgic. That was why Philo's doctrine of faith and the Logos, adopted by Ammonius Saccas as a substitute for the Christian, did not help Neo-Platonism to the truth. You remember the vivid picture, in Charles Kingsley's novel, of Hypatia's attempt to attain the intuition of Deity according to the Neo-Platonic formula, by the utter cessation of all conscious thought and the absorption of the soul for the instant into the Divinity; and you remember what, according to Kingsley, was its outcome. The representation is correct. From that quietistic phase, through all degrees, to the orgiastic phrenzy of the worshippers of Dionysus and Cybele on the one side, and to the hysteria of the revivalist, the trance of the " medium," or the *séance* of the spirit-rapper on the other, this idea has run its course; it has been the bond of union between false systems in every age; and large volumes might be written upon its various developments. Ancient Christianity always insisted that the true doctrine of Divine Communion and of Inspiration was differenced from the false, by the fact that a true inspiration and a true communion were acts of the conscious being; whereas the false inspiration was always marked by the endeavor to attain it through a state of excitement or quietism, terminating in unconsciousness—that is to say, by the trance of the medium, or the hysterics of the revival. The theology of the sacraments is the corrective of this aberration. Through the Church system, of which they are the centre, we enjoy the communion with God in Christ under the conditions of faith, worship, obedience, and sacramental participation, which appertain to the calling of the Christian from darkness to light, from error to truth, and from the power of Satan unto God.

When we turn from Clement of Alexandria to the study of the works of Origen, the first thing that strikes us is the strong common sense of the man, and with that, the vast reach of his mind, and the directness and force of his intellectual processes. Of his history and labors, the time at my command will not permit me to speak; and when I tell you that the article on Origen, in the lately published "Dictionary of Christian Biography," extends to forty-eight large and closely printed pages, besides fourteen pages on the controversy about his reputation after his death; and that the multitude of his writings has been said (no doubt erroneously) to be 6,000 in number, you will see that it is impossible to do him justice in a brief portion of one lecture.

What a teacher Origen was! Gregory Thaumaturgus, the Apostle of Armenia, was a pupil of his at Cæsarea after he had left Alexandria. On leaving school he delivered a valedictory address which was a panegyric upon his master, in which he tells us of his method. His first care was to make a careful study of the pupil himself, and to form his mind by a course in logic and dialectics. He noted his capacity, his faults, his tendencies, and applied the proper correctives, developing endurance, firmness, patience, thoroughness. He then led him to the "lofty and divine and most lovely" study of external nature, or natural science, as it was known to the ancient world. "He made Geometry the sure and immovable foundation, and from this rose step by step to the heights of heaven and the most sublime mysteries of the universe." Moral science came next; and here he laid the greatest stress upon the method of experiment. His life was a commentary upon his teaching. His own conduct was a more influential persuasive than argument, and by his example his scholars were enabled to perceive that the end of all was "to become like to God with a pure mind, and to draw near to Him and abide in Him." Then came Philosophy. His pupils were to examine the writings of philosophers and poets of every nation; for them there was to be no sect, no party; and in their arduous work they had a friend ever at hand in their master, who knew their difficulties and could guide them aright. So prepared, they were introduced to the study of Theology. "In the Holy Scriptures and the teaching of the Spirit, Origen found the final and absolute spring of Divine Truth." "Such," says Professor Westcott, "in meagre outline was, as Gregory tells us, the method of Origen. He describes what he knew, and what his hearers knew. There is no parallel to the picture in ancient times. And when every allowance has been made for the partial enthusiasm of a pupil, the view which it offers of a system of Christian training actually realized, exhibits a type which we [with our schools and universities and theological seminaries] cannot hope to surpass."

As a theologian and a witness to Church teaching, Origen, whatever mistakes he fell into, and however he has been represented or misrepresented in succeeding ages, desired and intended to be true to the principle which I have shown to be at the base of the School of Alexandria. The traditional Creed of the Church was his safeguard, and it is only as he overpassed that, that he is exposed to censure. In the preface to his *Principia* he says: " As we ceased to seek for truth among those who claimed it for erroneous opinions, after we had come to believe that Christ is the Son of God, and were persuaded that we must learn it from himself; so, seeing that there are many who think they hold the truth in Christ, but differ from their predecessors [we assert], since the teaching of the Church transmitted in orderly succession from the Apostles is preserved in the Churches to the present day, that that alone is to be accepted as truth which differs in no respect from ecclesiastical and apostolic tradition." He then gives a summary of Christian doctrine in the general order of the Creed, as the foundation of what he is about to say.

Instead of endeavoring to give you an estimate of Origen as a theologian, let me show you the man himself by an extract from his writings. Where in all theology will you find a grander passage than this, with which he introduces the discussion of the Incarnation of our blessed Lord? " But of all the mighty and marvellous acts related of Him, this altogether surpasses human admiration, and is beyond the power of mortal frailty to understand or feel: how that mighty power of Divine Majesty, that very Word of the Father, that very Wisdom of God, in whom were created all things visible and invisible, can be believed to have existed within the frame of that man who appeared in Judea; nay, that the Wisdom of God can have entered the womb, and have been born an infant, and have uttered wailings like the cries of a little child! And that afterward it should be said that He was greatly troubled, saying, ' My soul is sorrowful, even unto death;' and that at the last he was brought to that death which is accounted the most shameful among men—though He rose again the third day. Since, then, we see in Him some things so human that they differ in no respect from the common frailty of mortals, and some things so divine that they can belong to nothing else than the primal and ineffable nature of Deity, the narrowness of human understanding can find no outlet; but, overcome with the amazement of a mighty admiration, it knows not whither to retreat, or what to take hold of, or where to turn. If it think of a God, it sees a mortal; if it think of a man, it beholds him returning from the grave, having overthrown the empire of death and laden with its spoils. And therefore the spectacle is to be contemplated with all reverence, that the truth of both natures may be clearly shown to exist in one and the same being; so that nothing unworthy or unbecoming may be thought in that Divine and ineffable essence; nor yet those things which were done be supposed to be illusive and imaginary appearances. To utter these things in human ears, and to explain them in words, far surpasses the powers either of our rank, or of our intellect and language. I think that it surpasses the power even of the holy Apostles; nay, the explanation of the mystery may perhaps be beyond the grasp of the entire creation of celestial powers. Regarding Him, then, we shall state in the fewest words the contents of our creed, rather than the assertions of human reason."[1]

It was as an expositor of Holy Scripture that Origen was most renowned. His labors upon the text were remarkable for that age; he formed a collection of the various versions of the Old Testament, which was called the Hexapla, because it was arranged in six parallel columns; he is the first, or nearly the first, writer of commentaries; and Gregory tells us how pre-eminent he was as a lecturer upon the Bible. His method has been criticised as fanciful and dangerous; and yet it appears to me, from his explanation of it in the *Principia*, and when we compare it with the allegorism of Philo

[1] Origen: De Principiis, II. 6.

and Clement, to be marked with the strong common sense which I find in all Origen's writings, even when he is admittedly unsound; and to be in reality the method by which the true sense of Holy Scripture is ascertained. In the first place (and this is to be insisted upon), Origen endeavored to interpret Scripture according to the analogy of the faith and the tradition of the Church; and how important this principle was, at that time especially, can be known by seeing what the Gnostics made of Scripture when they interpreted it without this safeguard. Let me give you a simple instance. We, who are taught by the Nicene Creed, have no difficulty in understanding the first chapter of St. John's Gospel in its plain and natural sense: " In the beginning was the Word, and the Word was with God; and the Word was God," and the rest. But the Gnostics interpreted it something in this way: In a certain Being, whose name was Beginning, because he was the first of all, there was a certain Power called Word; and that Word was said to be with God, because He was the reflection of God in the mind of Beginning; and the Word was said to be God, because as the reflection he was the duplicate of God. And so when they came to the verse, " In Him was life, and the life was the light of men," they made out two more beings whose names were Light and Life, and so on.[1] In fact, if you would

[1] This is not scientifically exact, but sufficiently so for popular illustration.

THE SCHOOL OF ALEXANDRIA. 155

see a perfect *reductio ad absurdum* of the principle, "The Bible and the Bible only, without note or comment," you have only to look at the Gnostic expositions of Scripture in the eighth chapter of the first book of Irenæus against heresies. Against these follies the safeguard was the Creed and tradition of the Church. The other day I read, in a paper devoted to the task of proving that Christians ought to keep Saturday instead of Sunday, an article which was really quite able, showing that our blessed Lord was crucified on Wednesday, and rose from the dead on Saturday; and now that that idea is started, we shall probably hear more of it. What is the complete answer to that position? It is simply this, that the Church has kept Easter from the very beginning, and therefore cannot be uncertain as to the day of the week on which our Lord rose from the dead.[1] That is the value of the tradition of the Church in the interpretation of Scripture; and so Origen claims that he "clings to the standard of the heavenly Church of Jesus Christ according to the succession of the Apostles." Under this principle, Origen shows that there is a triple sense of

---

[1] The Quarto deciman controversy, instead of weakening, adds force to the tradition; a part of the Church keeping a day of the week, the other keeping the day of the month. There was no dispute either as to the day of the week or the day of the month. It was as if some kept Christmas always on the 25th December, and others on the Sunday nearest to that date.

Holy Scripture; and as he has to vindicate the unity of human nature against the Gnostics, he likens this triple sense to the tripartite nature of man, the *literal* sense corresponding to the bodily perceptions, the *psychical* or *moral* conveying instruction to the moral nature or soul, and the *mystical* or *spiritual* feeding the spirit, or religious nature. Now, although perhaps we do not speak in this way, yet there is no earnest and faithful preacher of the present day who does not attempt to draw from his text, in addition to its literal sense, the moral principle involved and the spiritual truth taught. Scripture *has* these three senses; and though it is true that the principle of mystical interpretation has been carried to fanciful lengths, yet it is recognized in the New Testament, especially in the Epistle to the Hebrews. Origen, however, is censured for saying that certain passages in Scripture do not contain the " corporeal " or literal sense—by which he is thought to mean that they are not literally and historically true, and so to discredit the integrity of the record. It is possible that he may be open to that censure; but if we look at the examples he gives in the fourth book of the *Principia* to illustrate his meaning, I think we may relieve him of it by understanding him rightly. For example, he tells us that certain Jews refused to believe in our Lord because they did not find that prophecy *literally* fulfilled after His advent—that the wolf was to feed with the lamb, and the leopard to lie down with the kid, and the calf and the young lion and the fatling together, and a little child to lead them. Again, he anticipates modern objections to the first chapter of Genesis, by showing that the first three days of creation could not be literal days—that is, days of sunlight followed or preceded by moonlight or darkness—because they passed before the sun and moon were set as lights in the heavens. So he says: " Cain, when going forth from the presence of the Lord, certainly appears to thoughtful men as likely to lead the reader to inquire what is the presence of God, and what is meant by going out from it." So also, we are not to understand *literally*, that the devil, taking our Lord up into a high mountain, showed to his bodily eye all the kingdoms of the world and the glory of them; because there is no mountain so high that they could possibly be visible from it. One other example I must give to illustrate Origen's acuteness and hard common sense; the injunction, "If anyone smite thee on the right cheek, turn to him the other also," was not intended to be literally understood, " because he who strikes, unless he has some bodily defect, smites the *left* cheek with the *right* hand." I am not learned in what remains of Origen's expository works, and cannot tell how far he sacrificed the letter; but certainly, as illustrated by these examples, and within these limits, I hold the principle to be sound. No one can have studied the Fathers of the Church without being profoundly impressed with the wealth of meaning they find in Holy Scripture, when they make use judiciously of that principle of type and prefiguration of which we are unjustly suspicious when we find it called "mystical." Melchizedek was a type of Christ; so was Isaac bearing the wood for the sacrifice; so was Joseph sold into Egypt; so was Joshua leading the people over Jordan; so was David establishing the kingdom of God in Israel; so was Solomon building the temple; so was Jonah; so were others; and as they were types, so may their history be interpreted as prophecies of Christ and shadows of heavenly things.

But Origen, though he did not intend to depart in any way from Catholic tradition, and the faith of the Church, stands as a beacon of warning to the theologians of later times, and as an illustration to us of the remark already quoted, that the marriage of religion with philosophy is the marriage of an immortal with a mortal, and that, while the religion lives, the philosophy dies away. In his statement of the truths attested by Christian tradition in the preface to the *Principia*, Origen remarks that certain points were not clearly defined in the teaching of the Church, and therefore that inquiry was admissible and necessary in order to arrive at the proper conclusions respecting them. That inquiry he pursues, not dogmatically, but as a deliberation, and he expressly tells his reader that he must make up his own mind as to the value of his opinions. But it is just here that no one can follow him; and no one can follow him here, because his opinions rest upon an adulteration of Catholic teaching with the current philosophy. Just at the time that Origen was rising to eminence, Neo-Platonism was attracting attention; and in his large-minded desire to know all that could be known, Origen attended the lectures of Ammonius Saccas. From his philosophical studies Origen derived the ideas of a succession of worlds; of the pre-existence of souls; of a previous probation of souls, by which he accounted, not only for the inequalities of birth, fortune, happiness, and capacity of human beings in this life, but for the different ranks and orders of the spiritual world, good and evil; and of a state of indefinite discipline and progression by which all souls might be reclaimed and restored at last. Resulting from these ideas, he held a doctrine of free-will which might be cited as Pelagian by anticipation; and carried his speculations so far as to suppose that the soul of our blessed Lord merited the union with Deity in the incarnation by the faith and love with which it clung to God in the pre-existent state, when all other souls fell away in a greater or less degree. The passage in which Origen develops this idea is, for its religious tone, one of the most beautiful in the *Principia*, but, beautiful as it is, it is baseless and dangerous; the idea is borrowed from philosophy, and perverts the texts of Scripture which Origen cites in its support. Hence it was, by the union of conclusions drawn from philosophy with conclusions securely founded on the faith of the Church, that Origen, though one of the greatest Catholic teachers, and not at all a heretic either in intent or fact, nevertheless furnishes in his writings so much that is unsound as to permit almost every subsequent heresy to support itself by his authority. This accounts for the violent controversy which raged about his memory in the subsequent ages; and this is the reason why his name stands as the warning to those who adulterate the pure truth of the Word with the opinions, or the philosophy, or the science, that are current in any particular age. When philosophy is finished, and when science is complete, then the harmony of religion with philosophy and science will be self-evident, and need no demonstration; as long as philosophy and science are progressive and approximate, the key-stone that sustains the arch which joins them with theology cannot be put in place. One of the foundations is lacking, though the other is firm and sure. Where Origen expounded the Catholic faith, his work is as valuable now as ever; where he based opinions upon philosophy there is no thinker now, Catholic or heterodox, who will avow himself his disciple.

The great reputation of Origen as a teacher caused him to be sought after to refute heresy in widely separated localities; but it was under his friend and pupil Dionysius, who, after being head of the Catechetical school, was made Bishop in 247, that the Alexandrian Church began to exercise that ecumenical influence which in due time enabled Athanasius to conquer the Arian heresy. With Dionysius learning ascended the Episcopal throne; but the learning of Dionysius was not more conspicuous than the loving nature of the man, and his broad and sympathetic mind. The time was one of great difficulty; the Decian and Valerian persecutions occurred in his episcopate; Rome was harassed by the Sabellian heresy and the Novatian schism; the Church of Antioch by the worldliness of Paul of Samosata; and the Alexandrian Church by carnal and materialistic notions of the life after the Resurrection. Dionysius brought his influence to bear through the whole Church for peace and truth and right. His Episcopal correspondence was great, and his temper always kindly. Only fragments of his writings remain, but they show that controversy was not always acrimonious, and that to speak the truth in love is the way to win over those who are in error.

It does not fall within the plan of this lecture to carry on the history into and beyond the Nicene age, and I cannot do more than speak the names of S. Athanasius and S. Cyril, those great champions of the Church against the Arian and Nestorian heresies. One remark which has been made about S. Athanasius I must not permit to pass unnoticed. "His name," it has been said, "stands for the encouragement of those who resist the Church in the interest of some higher truth which it has not yet learned to appreciate; his experience illustrates that one man standing out against the Church may be right, and the Church may be wrong; and further, his life demonstrates how at all critical moments the faith takes refuge, not in institutions, but in individual men." The remark is not original with the author of the book from which I make this quotation; but, borrowed or original, it would have been repudiated at once by Athanasius himself. He would have been the last man in the world to allow himself to be taken for the example and justification of any precocious juvenile who may set himself up to be wiser than the Church of God. It is indeed true that, in critical moments, God in His goodness does raise up some great and commanding character to uphold the witness of His Church to the faith; but this sentence, as an interpretation of Athanasius's place in Church history, is wholly wrong. The old phrase was not *Athanasius contra ecclesiam*, but *Athanasius contra mundum*. At one time, indeed, when the pressure of the imperial will was too strong for men of less heroic temper than himself, he seemed to stand alone; but it is not true that at any time the free voice of the Church was against him; or that the heart and soul of the thousands and ten thousands of Christendom were not with him in his noble contention for the faith once delivered to the saints.

One question concerning the Alexandrian Church has pressed upon my mind in considering its eventful history. How was it that so great and noble a Church as this was in the first five centuries, should have sunk so low in after-ages? I do not know that I can give the answer; but I have the opinion that one defect in its theology contributed to it. Notwithstanding the immense service it rendered to the Church Universal in vindicating the Divine side of the doctrine of the Incarnation, it seems to me that the Alexandrian Church had an insufficient appreciation of the human side of that mystery, and a resulting feebleness in apprehending the sacramental relation of the Christian to Christ Incarnate in the economy of redemption. Required by their relation to the Gnostic heresies, and the Arian and Nestorian impieties, to vindicate the deity of the Son, and the universal influence of the Logos in creation and in humanity, the Alexandrian Fathers paid less attention to the special relation into which the believing Christian is brought to the Redeemer, through the sacramental communion with Him as the Head and Restorer of fallen human nature. It is startling, when we remember the Monophysite controversies of the fifth century, to come across the following passage in the *Stromata* of Clement, as early as the beginning of the third century: "The [true] Gnostic is such that he is subject only to the affections which exist for the maintenance of the body, such as hunger, thirst, and the like. But in the case of the Saviour it were foolish to suppose that the body, as a body, demanded the necessary aids in order to its duration. For He ate, not for the sake of the body, which was kept together by a holy energy, but in order that it might not enter into the minds of those who were with Him, to entertain a different opinion of Him; as certainly some afterward supposed that He appeared in a phantasmal shape. But He was entirely impassible; inaccessible to any movement of feeling, either pleasure or pain."[1] That is not true. He was an hungered; He was athirst; He said, "My soul is exceeding sorrowful, even unto death;" He was "in all points tempted like as we are, yet without sin." It is not true, and the results of the teaching founded upon it were disastrous to the Alexandrian Church. The idea of an impassive Christ, accepted as the ideal of Egyptian monasticism, reacted to promote the acceptance of the Monophysite heresy, when the imperial power attempted to enforce the decrees of Chalcedon against the patriarch Dioscorus. Under this influence the Coptic portion of the Egyptian patriarchate broke with the Church and the Empire, made a feeble resistance to their enemies, accepted the Mohammedan domination, and was ground down beneath its iron heel.

And this may teach us of the present day that the Christian Faith, delivered in its integrity at the beginning, and witnessed to by the continuous and consentient testimony of the Church of all ages, is

[1] Stromata, B. VI., ch. 9.

greater than any particular school of thought; and that, so far from theological schools having "developed" it into something more than it was at first, there is no particular school which has adequately explained it. You may understand what I mean by considering a fact which is within the experience of a devout Christian layman. Such an one, believing as he does the Creed in its fulness, though unable to explain his thought in theological terms, hears perhaps some able discourse in which he instinctively detects a false note. He may not be able to explain why, but he is sure that the objective faith is greater and higher than the explanation of it. So it is with schools of thought in the Church. The faith itself is greater than the thought of the particular school—the *implicit* faith, to speak scholastically, is more full and profound than the explicit faith. Now, the great defect in the theological training of to-day, especially outside the Church, is that it is more given to a subjective analysis of thought about the Creed than to an objective study of the Creed itself; and therefore, after reading much of that kind of writing, especially if it emanates from Germany, the impression left is dreamy and unreal. We believe, if we are Christians, not in what Clement or Origen, or even Athanasius and Cyril, thought about God; we believe in God. And the study of their thoughts is useful so far as it leads us to believe in God more firmly, and not otherwise; so far as it leads us to see that, underlying all the differences of different schools of thought and modes of expression, there are the objective truths of the faith once delivered to the saints.

And yet schools of thought are inevitable in the Church; and if they accept the whole Creed, and differ only in the perspective, so to speak, with which it groups itself about the special truth that is most vividly realized in particular circumstances, they are altogether beneficial, and help to the realization of the whole faith by the whole Church. Let me endeavor to illustrate again from personal experience. One man receives the whole Creed in its integrity, but the special truth in it which appeals most strongly to his Christian consciousness is the Fatherhood of God. He groups the whole Creed around that truth, and thus develops a particular school of thought. Another apprehends as the central truth of the Creed for him—as the truth which meets his personal conviction of sin—the doctrine of the Atonement; around that, then, he groups the whole Creed, and develops another school of thought. A third apprehends, as the vital truth in his experience, the ever-present grace of God's Holy Spirit; that furnishes the stand-point for a third school of thought. A fourth takes his stand upon the Incarnation and the Sacraments, grouping the whole Creed around these truths, as those which are realized most intently in his experience, and so there is formed a fourth school of thought. Now, all these are real schools of Christian thought; and they may coexist in the Church in entire harmony, because the Church's faith includes the central principles of them all; and the more truly Catholic the Church is, the more harmoniously they will coexist in its bosom.

But it must be evident, from this illustration, that the Catholicity of any of these schools of thought rests in the mutual communion of them all with one another in the unity of the Church. The most Catholic-minded Christian will be he—if there be one large-minded enough—who can realize in his own experience, with equal force and vividness, the central truth of each and all these separate schools; because they are all founded on vital truths of the Creed itself. Now, the influence of unity in the one communion is to produce this result—to supplement the one-sidedness of the particular development by the comprehensive catholicity which results from the harmony of all. The history of the General Councils is the grand illustration of this power. But if the school of thought is not content with thus apprehending the Creed, as related to its own experience, but denies the point of view of other schools, and endeavors to cramp all Christian experience to its own narrow measure, then it ceases to be a *school*, and becomes a *party;* and though the school is beneficial, the party is altogether hurtful. No matter what its foundation, it is narrow and schismatical in temper, unjust in its judgments, uncatholic in its methods, and incapable of a real advance in the knowledge of the things of God. What then must be the result, when the *party* becomes a *sect*, splits off from the communion of the Church, and gathers to itself only those who are like-minded, but to stereotype its narrowness, to ossify its heart, and to fossilize its brain.

The condition of rising to the height and expanding to the fulness of Christian truth is to be in living, sympathetic communion with the whole Church of all ages, that which is *semper, ubique et ab omnibus;* within whose organization, One, Holy, Catholic and Apostolic, all differences are minimized, all truths are harmonized, and all the members have full scope for the exercise of their various gifts in communion with each other, and in loyal fidelity to the Head ; who provided for this in the institution of His Church, when " He gave some, apostles; and some, prophets ; and some, pastors and teachers ; for the perfecting of the saints, for the work of the ministry, for the edifying of the body of Christ ; till we all come, in the unity of the faith, and of the knowledge of the Son of God, unto a perfect man, unto the measure of the stature of the fulness of Christ."

The Church of Rome in her Relation to Christian Unity.

LECTURE V.

THE RIGHT REV. GEO. F. SEYMOUR, S.T.D., LL.D.,
Bishop of Springfield.

THE CHURCH OF ROME IN HER RELATION TO CHRISTIAN UNITY.

PREFACE.

A FEW words are necessary to put the reader in possession of facts which he ought to know, in justice as well to the writer as to himself.

The Church Club of New York honored the lecturer with an invitation to deliver an Address on the subject of " The Papacy in its Relation to Christian Unity." He accepted, and intended to write out in full what he had to say, but the press of work in his diocese, and other duties, prevented. Accordingly he was obliged to address his audience, on the 8th of May last, without a single note. When the lecture was ended, the lecturer supposed that his work was done. But he was doomed to disappointment. The Club desired to print the Lectures, and would not consent to omit the one on Rome, hence the unhappy lecturer was forced to reproduce on paper what he had some days before—two full weeks—uttered by word of mouth. The only time he could command for this purpose was while crossing the Atlantic on the steamer; since, immediately on reaching Europe, other engagements claimed him, without interruption, until his return, in the autumn, to America.

Under the above circumstances the Lecture has been prepared for publication—away from books, on the bosom of the deep. The lecturer does not seek to deprecate criticism, but he would suggest to those who are disposed to be censorious, that it might be worth their while first to try their hand at preparing an historic lecture without a single book of reference, and with the accompaniment of ocean waves, a rolling steamer, and friends and neighbors on all sides prostrate with sea-sickness. The writer has tried to present the substance of what he said on the evening of the 8th of May, 1888, in Christ Church, New York City, and he trusts that his memory has been true in the facts and dates which he has set down under its instruction. About his argument he feels no doubt whatsoever.

G. F. S.

STEAMER "GERMANIC," AT SEA,
June 1, 1888.

LECTURE.

There is no name with which a student of the past can conjure more successfully than with that of Rome. Whether he proposes to deal with secular or ecclesiastical history the word is equally potent. It represents what fills a larger sphere in either field of research than any other. There are cities which perchance can challenge comparison with Rome in the one or the other of these departments of history *alone*, but there is none which can approach her in *both*.

When one utters the magic name, "Rome," he throws a spell upon memory. The past gives up its treasures. A panorama passes before the mind, which reproduces a period of nearly three thousand years, and illustrates the fortunes of mankind, as they grow and advance and reach down from century to century, and come at length to us, who are living here to-day, in speech, and customs, and laws, and institutions, and religion, and with some in superstitions. The contemplation of this double life of Rome, her secular and ecclesiastical history, places us abreast of our subject, assigned us by the Church Club of New York, to discuss in your presence to-night, "The Relation of the Papacy to the Recovery of Christian Unity."

We cannot meet this question without taking into view the career of Rome antecedent to the birth of Christ, and her relative position among the nations of the earth at the day of Pentecost ; since, as we shall presently see, these facts constitute *the suggestion*, we may say *the inspiration* of Papal aggrandizement and usurpation as embodied now in the polity administered by Leo XIII.

It is interesting in the highest degree, as an abstract study, to note the origin of Rome in the smallest of small beginnings, with the fortunes of the Twins, and to trace its progress through the mist of fable and legend until we emerge at length in company with a State which has already attained respectable proportions in territory and population, and developed the principles which are destined to contribute in a larger degree than anything else to its almost uninterrupted success on the lines of growth, consolidation, and conquest. The Roman, we discover, was born to obey as well as to rule, and hence the individual imparts to the national life his own characteristics, and builds up institutions, civil and military, which embody pre-eminently the ideas of order, law, discipline, subordination, and organization.

Were we to place before the eye a series of maps, representing the world of the ancients from the eighth century before Christ, century by century, down to the date of our Saviour's birth, we would see the City of the Seven Hills, as map replaced map, enlarging its domain, gradually at first, then by rapid strides, advancing steadily, grasping, and holding as it grasped, province after province, kingdom after kingdom, nation after nation, until the map which closed the series, and spread before our astonished gaze the earth as it existed politically when Jesus dwelt among us in the flesh, would show us the entire circle of civilized peoples tributary to Rome. Her arm on the right had swept to the North and the East and the South, and brought the countries which Alexander had conquered beneath her sway; her arm on the left had rested upon Gaul, Southern Germany, Hispania, and more distant Britain, and reaching down beyond the Pillars of Hercules and the Mediterranean Sea, had laid hold of Mauritania and Numidia, and joined the conquests which she had made in the East and the South to those which she had achieved in the North and the West. The little speck, not larger apparently than a man's hand, on the banks of the Tiber in the eighth century before the Christian era, had grown through the intervening ages until it covered the whole face of the earth when Augustus reigned. The period of the kings, the local conflicts with surrounding tribes, the invasion of the Gauls, the Samnite and Punic wars, the wars of Jugurtha and Pompey and Cæsar, will serve as indices to mark her advance and help us to chronicle the progress of Rome toward universal empire.

The earth has never seen such an empire before or since, and doubtless never will again. Relatively to the population then living it was immeasurably the greatest. In point of territory it filled the whole *orbis terrarum* of civilized mankind, and went beyond, and exacted submission from barbarous tribes which occupied the border lands between light and darkness, the races which we know, and the fabulous creatures which legend presents as dwelling in the extremities of the world. It was not alone, nor chiefly the population, nor the territory of the Roman Empire which made her great, but her organization, her unity. Rome, the City, summed up the Empire; she was the heart, the soul of the huge domain; she was the centre, from her radiated all power, and all looked to her for protection. She sealed her conquests, at her discretion, with the signet ring of her franchise, and Asiatic and African, as well as European, became *Roman citizens*. The title was no empty name, witness the invective of Cicero, note the appeal of Saul of Tarsus in the prison at Philippi. Rome unified the world as she strode out and on from Italy in the march of victory; she made her tributaries, in a sense more than nominal, "*Roman.*" They received the impress of her spirit and institutions, and in return they made their contribution to enhance her greatness. She was the mistress of the world, and was acknowledged as such from the Indus to the Atlantic Ocean.

There were great cities before Rome, there have been great cities since; there are great, no doubt greater cities now, but Rome at the time the Church of Christ was begotten by the Holy Ghost on the day of Pentecost was unparalleled and unapproachable in its greatness. It was the first city of the world *in every department of human endeavor, and in every element of material greatness*. Other cities have excelled in population, in commerce, in arts, in manufactures, in finance, in worldliness, and, we may add, in wickedness and sin; in some one or more of these characteristics individual cities, which can be named, have ranked first, or are now accounted pre-eminent. Rome at the time of which we speak was *facile princeps* in all. She was the seat of universal empire, her armies were in all the world, along her *Via Sacra* marched triumphal processions, which displayed trophies and captives from every clime. No census tells the exact number of people who dwelt in her houses and occupied her suburbs, but the ruins, which lie around, and stretch away for many miles from the Forum and the Capitol, proclaim a population of at least a million. Her shops, her busy streets, the noise and din of many crafts exhibit her industries and tell of the activity and volume of her trade and commerce. The elegancies of life were there in all their superfluity, luxuries which minister to the senses, and delights which gratify the taste and ravish the imagination. And there, too, the world, in the darkest phases of its rebellion against God, and light and truth and morals, stood forth in gigantic proportions, regardless of shame and defying restraint. Rome was indeed what her own sad, desponding historian describes her as being, the "*cloaca maxima*," the mighty sewer into which the wickedness of the whole world was poured.

Let us look off from Rome on another scene. The place is a hill, not the Mons Palatinus, but the Mount of Ascension, and the figures on whom we gaze are not Romulus and his followers, but the King of Kings and His Apostles. The occasion is not the founding of an earthly city, but the setting up of the heavenly kingdom. Our Lord, in the supreme moment of His sojourn among men, as His final act, with His last words, is giving to His disciples the plenary charter of their ministry, and prescribing the fundamental and essential principles of the constitution of His Church. The fourth great empire, as sketched by the Prophet Daniel, has now reached the zenith of its power, and the fifth, the final kingdom, against which the gates of hell shall not prevail, is coming to its birth. The King in disguise, for the infinite God is hidden beneath the form of the Son of Man—the King in disguise is taking order for the government and administration of His kingdom by deputation, until He shall come again in the same nature, but no longer disguised, at the end of the world. Nothing can be more sublimely awful than the quiet and seclusion and majesty of our Lord's preparation for the birth of His Church. Were it not for the revelation of the Blessed Spirit we would know nothing of those momentous occurrences and words on which depended the organism and character of the kingdom of God on earth. Hence the tremendous significance of the disclosure made in the closing verses of S. Matthew's Gospel. It gathers, as it were, into a focus, all that had gone before of Christ's commands to His disciples, as touching their office, and it adds, besides, the basis of the authority on which they were to rest in the discharge of duty, further powers filling out the entire sphere of delegated administration which they were to exercise until His return, and the limitations under which they were to act and work. Remember, for we cannot emphasize too strongly the facts upon which we are now dwelling, they are crucial in any discussion of the polity of the Christian Church, they enter as a question antecedent to all others in any thought of Christian unity which embraces the Patriarchate of Rome as a party. The Holy Ghost admits us to the seclusion of our Lord's final interview with His Apostles ere He steps and passes from earth to heaven; He allows us to share in hearing *His last words* spoken in this world to the Eleven, before He seats Himself upon His mediatorial throne in the sky. This fact is of transcendent importance. It takes us into partnership with the Apostles, and makes us privy to the principles upon which they were to build and administer the Church, which was soon to come into existence.

Our Lord, we note, "leads His Apostles out as far as to Bethany." As he had originally chosen them and appointed them their place, and reminded them from time to time that they were called with a vocation, and were acting under direction, as when He said, "I appoint unto you a kingdom," or again, "Ye have not chosen Me, but I have chosen you, and ordained you, that ye should go and bring forth fruit, and that your fruit should remain," so now at the end, "He leads them out," separates them from the rest of men, and orders them, as He would have them, each in his place, and sets them before His face, that He may look at them and address them. The circumstance that "He led them out," the circumstance that He regulated their position ere He delivered to them His final commission, His last commands, adds weight, if anything could, to His words; helps to interpret, if anything were needed to make more plain, the meaning of His behest. The Holy Spirit paints for us the scene, He rehearses for us the words. What we see, and what we hear, harmonize, produce one impression, and that the deepest which could be made. And this, we are bold to say, is the purpose of the Holy Ghost. He aims to protect with all the safeguards which divine foresight could provide, the polity of His Church. Inspiration, it would seem, could do no more than to bring mankind as spectators and witnesses of the giving of the charter, the drafting of the constitution of Christ's Kingdom on earth. Inspiration, it would seem, could do no more than to lead us along through the first years of the Church's life with her, as she grows and develops and spreads abroad, and show us how the Apostles, who saw and heard their Lord, understood Him and executed His commands. We see the grouping, we read the charter, and we are permitted to learn the manner in which the original officers appointed under that charter by Jesus Christ Himself interpreted its meaning and carried out its provisions. The final verses of S. Matthew's Gospel give us the charter, the Acts of the Holy Apostles exhibit for five-and-twenty years the practical administration of government under that charter by those to whom the Sovereign Himself gave it. Could we ask for further information to make us certain as to the character of the polity of the Church? Are we at a loss to answer whether the King committed the administration of His Kingdom *to a single vicegerent, or to a corporation;* whether he organized its government on earth *as an oligarchy under Him, or an absolute monarchy on a level with Him?* On this point there can be no doubt at all if we accept the testimony of Holy Scripture; not the evidence of a single verse, or the inference gathered from isolated texts, but the very charter itself, given by our Lord Himself in His very words, and the practical interpretation put upon that charter by all of those who first received office under it, without exception, to the end of their lives, in the organization of the churches which they planted, and the teaching which they gave to their followers. No answer but one has ever been given dogmatically to the question—in whom did our Lord lodge the government of His Church, in one or several; did He vest its offices and functions and powers in a single vicar, or in a corporation? No answer save one has ever been given as a matter of faith by any branch of the Church, until the Patriarchate of Rome, in the year of grace 1870, in the dogma of infallibility, presumed to affirm and require all who owned her obedience to accept as *de fide* that Christ constituted His Church an absolute monarchy, that he appointed S. Peter His vicar, raising him above his fellows into an order by himself, and lodged in him and his successors all power for government and administration.

It is true that from an early period the ideas of centralization, unification, and supremacy began to take shape and form in the mind of the West, and Rome of course naturally lent itself to give expression to these ideas, and translate them, as it was most plausibly believed and maintained, for the benefit of mankind, into a blessed reality. The process was very gradual, and in its course of onward progress and development it had its perturbations and recessions; but still, on the whole, the growing power advanced, and making use of what

RELATION TO CHRISTIAN UNITY. 183

it had obtained by concession, by tentative claim, by haughty demand, as a foothold, it leaped to loftier pretensions, and then made good by persistent assertion, in the face of ignorance and incapacity to obtain the requisite information for refutation, its extravagant demands upon the obedience of mankind. We can readily trace the advance of Victor beyond Soter, of Julius beyond Victor, of Leo the Great beyond Julius, of Gregory the Great beyond Leo the Great, of Gregory II. and III. beyond their illustrious predecessor, of the seventh Gregory beyond all that had gone before him, of Innocent III. in advance of Gregory, of Boniface VIII. still further on in the career of self-assertion and unfounded claim. Still, while the Patriarch of Rome is thus practically, in the minds and before the eyes of men, growing away from all other bishops, and lifting his head above his fellows, and crowning himself with a triple crown, he does not impose the system upon the world as a Divine institution to be accepted, as a matter of faith, under the penalty of excommunication. Centuries drift on, and it is reserved for our time and the present generation to see this result reached. In 1870 the decree of infallibility was formulated and proclaimed as an article of faith by Pius IX. From that hour and henceforth the Patriarchate of Rome becomes responsible for revolutionizing the policy of the Christian Church as established by Christ, and administered by His Apostles and their colleagues and successors. This is an awful charge to make, and no one should presume to present such an indictment unless he has at his command ample proof to sustain it. Fortunately, in good measure, our duty on this line is already discharged before we formulate and make our assertion.

It only remains that we should bring together and contrast the two systems—namely, *first*, the polity revealed by S. Matthew in recording the acts and words of our Blessed Lord, and by S. Luke in narrating the history of the administration of the Church by His Apostles; and, *secondly*, the polity as now received and imposed by the Church of Rome. The one is a government entrusted *to a corporation*, the other is an *absolute monarchy ruled by one ;* the former is limited by a prescribed charter with terms and conditions, the latter supersedes all charters human and divine, and stands on its own naked authority without condition or limit. The first lodges all ministerial power and official grace in the hands of eleven, who are to act in co-ordination, in mutual dependence upon each other; the second makes a single man the reservoir of all God's spiritual gifts to the Church, and the sole dispenser of official dignity and sacramental blessing. Let us look on the two pictures, the one of Christ and His Apostles, photographed for us by the light of the Holy Spirit; the other of the Pope and his cardinals, present before our eyes to-day, as falling within the sphere of our own personal knowledge and experience.

Christ, after the resurrection, when the forty days had come to an end, when it was time for Him to ascend into Heaven, where He was before He became incarnate, but not as He was before, but now with our humanity vindicated from the curse of the law, purged from sin, and triumphant over death and the grave, indissolubly united to His divine Person—Christ, as He was thus about to leave this world, not to appear again until He shall come with power and great glory to judge the quick and the dead, makes final provision for the setting up His kingdom on earth and its continuance and administration during the interval until His return. His acts and words are supremely important; of course they always are, but a distinction may be taken, and some in the very nature of the words and acts themselves are of greater gravity and weight than others. If we allow this difference, and without the least approach to irreverence practically we must, among the most solemn things which Jesus ever did and said are those which immediately precede His ascension. They are *His last acts, His last words.* The Holy Ghost summons all the world through S. Matthew and S. Luke to behold and listen. What do we see and hear? Jesus leads His Apostles out, not *one* but *all*, as far as to Bethany. There, *in the midst of them*, He makes known to them His will touching them and their relation to Him, and under Him to His kingdom the Church. The words are few, but they are pregnant with meaning, and settle for ever decisively and irrevocably the principles of the government of His Church throughout all time. "He led them out as far as to Bethany" (S. Luke xxiv. 20). "And Jesus came and spake unto them, saying, All power is given unto Me in heaven and in earth. Go ye therefore, and teach all nations, baptizing them in the name of the Father, and of the Son, and of the Holy Ghost. Teaching them to observe all things, whatsoever I have commanded you; and lo, I am with you alway, even unto the end of the world" (S. Matt. xxviii. 18–20). Here we see and hear, as the deliberate will of our risen Lord, that He entrusts His kingdom to *a corporation*. He plans to do so, He leads them, He draws near to them, and addresses them collectively. These acts are the deliberate expression of His will, they show His settled purpose and design. Then His words are in harmony with His acts. He speaks to them as *a body*, He uses the *plural number*, "Go ye," "baptize ye," "teach ye," "lo, I am with you" (plural). When He willed He could select, and separate, and speak to one, and pass by the rest. Jesus could draw S. John to His side; He could single out S. Thomas and address him by name; He could challenge S. Peter three times in the presence of his fellow-disciples with the question, "Lovest thou Me more than these?" He could as well, had He so willed, have addressed His plenary commission of government and administration on the Mount of Ascension to S. Peter, *but He did not do so*, although S. Peter was there. He delivered the charter on the contrary, containing all the powers and all the limitations, to all the Apostles together, including S. Peter, as a body, to have and to hold the trust in common in co-ordination. It is indeed the plenary commission, since our Lord provides for all men and for all time and for the entire spheres of teaching and duty. He assigns them their jurisdiction : " All nations." He forecasts the duration of their ministry : " Lo, I am with you alway, even unto the end of the world." He prescribes the subject-matter of their instruction : " Teaching them to observe all things whatsoever I have commanded you." He imposes limitations ; He restrains them by associating them together and making them mutually dependent upon each other, so that no one should go beyond and defraud his brethren by self-assertion and self-will, but all should act in co-ordination and in subjection to His sovereign will. They are to teach and enjoin obedience, but the delegated power is conditioned by the proviso, " whatsoever I have commanded you."

When we pass from the Mount of Ascension to the day of Pentecost and the first years of the Church's life, we are permitted by the Blessed Spirit to study the administration of the Apostles, acting under the charter which, as we have just seen, they received as a *joint commission* from their Lord. Their understanding of their Divine Master's words as expressed by their teaching and the execution of their trust must be, it would seem to us, decisive of the polity of Christ's Church, and the more emphatically so, because we have in their conduct in these regards not alone the consensus of a body of devout, intelligent men, but the united and unanimous witness of a body of such men *inspired by the Blessed Spirit*. Could anything be stronger than such an attestation of the character of the polity of Christ's Church being in accordance with His will: it will suffice for our purpose to look at the front ranks of the Christian army, those who were enrolled and were drilled by the Apostles themselves and their associates. These surely must be right as regards all the essentials of faith and practice. If these, *the first-fruits of the Spirit*, marching under the orders and the eyes of the Twelve, are radically and fundamentally in error, we confess that we lose hope, and surrender in despair. The Holy Ghost casts the bright beams of His illumination upon the very first believers, and brings them out from the oblivion of the past, and sets them before us that we may look at them and take them for our examples. The description is vivid, comprehensive, and decisive as touching the polity of the Church while these men lived and when they died, and many of them, most of them, sealed their testimony of their love and obedience with their blood. The record of these, *the very first believers*, set down in Holy Scripture is, "they continued steadfastly in the Apostles' doctrine and fellowship, and in breaking of bread and in prayers" (Acts ii. 42).

These believers, three thousand in number, represent the mind and teaching of S. Peter and his associates. They tell us by their steadfast behavior, more plainly than words could do so, what their teachers, and what they, as taught, understood the polity of Christ's Church to be—precisely what our Lord prescribed, a government taking oversight of faith and practice, of teaching and sacraments and devotion, vested in a corporation ; for it is declared by the Blessed Spirit that these first Christians continued steadfastly in the *Apostles*', *not S. Peter's* doctrine and fellowship, " and in breaking of bread and in prayers." We have before us, placed there by the Holy Ghost, the charter of Christ's Church in His own precious words ; we have the first officers appointed under the provisions of that charter by the Divine Master in person, and we have those officers in the actual administration of their trust, under the guidance of the Blessed Spirit, preaching, teaching, baptizing, confirming, celebrating the Holy Eucharist, exercising discipline, ordaining, and governing in Christ's name ; and the polity, the form of government as set down in our Lord's own words, as understood and accepted and administered by those who heard those words, and who were guided into all truth by the Holy Ghost, and as received and steadfastly obeyed by those who were so taught by the Apostles and their associates, *is a corporate government, vested in a body of men,* eleven at first, then twelve, and then multiplying along the line of the same order, the highest in the sacred ministry, until the needs of all nations were supplied and continuing to the end of the world. This is clear if anything is clear, and can be made clear.

The form of Church government which exists now in the Patriarchate of Rome as a matter of fact *is an absolute monarchy,* unlimited from beneath, and scarcely, if at all, limited from above. The Bishop of Rome in the theory of the Vatican decrees, which supersede the charter of Christ, is more autocratic than any earthly monarch has ever been, or in the nature of things can be. He is above all, he rules all, and is ruled by none. In his solitary grandeur he sits above all who reign and govern in this world on his lonely throne, and when he speaks as Pope in the sphere of faith and morals his voice is the infallible voice of God. His jurisdiction reaches from pole to pole, it embraces all lands, and all the islands of the sea. He has, and can have, no colleague, no companion. His powers are incommunicable, save to a successor, and a successor can only appear *after he is dead.* He is an order by himself, and his exaltation sinks the apostolate out of the place which Christ gave it into a grade of the priesthood. This is the polity of the Patriarchate of Rome as formulated and imposed by the Vatican Council of 1870.

As we look on Christ's charter and then on this scheme of government, we are forced to the conclusion that they are irreconcilable absolutely and hopelessly. There have been, sometime and somewhere, usurpation, subversion, and revolution. The Vatican form of Church polity is not a product of Christ's charter. It is *a perversion of it*, a radical and fundamental change, involving a rooting up of principles and the substitution of other and essentially different principles. For example, Christ made His Church catholic, the Twelve, as the Revelation of S. John informs us, look, three to the north, three to the south, three to the east, and three to the west; they form a hollow square, and face the four quarters of the earth, the entire circle of humanity, and to these, not to one, *but to all*, the risen Lord gave commission, *on an equality*, that they might go forward and convert the nations and draw them to look up to the King over all in heaven, the incarnate Lord on His throne, the Sun of Righteousness who shines for all. Rome destroys catholicity, and makes the Church *local, Roman*, as God made His ancient Church *national, Jewish*. God's purpose was, as revealed by the prophets, out of the shell of Judaism, local, national, narrow, to produce the tree which should cover the whole earth, the Christian Church, catholic, universal, for all lands, for all peoples, stamped with the impress of no one to the exclusion of the others, but equally the property of all, appropriated by each, and yet at home everywhere, just as the sun in the sky shines for all, belongs to all, without invading the proprietorship of each in him as a private possession, so that men say, without prejudice to the rights and claims of others, an American sun, an English sun, an Italian sun, a tropical sun, an Arctic sun. Thus by Christ's charter and constitution the Church is catholic, equally at home in all lands, and yet the exclusive possession of none: the Oriental Catholic Church for the Orient, the Occidental Catholic Church for the Occident, the Roman Catholic Church for Italy, the Anglo-Catholic Church for England, the Canadian Catholic Church for Canada, and the American Catholic Church for the United States; but at the same time there are not a plurality of Catholic Churches, for that would be an absurdity, but *one Catholic Church*, even as there are not many suns, *but one sun*. Rome by her present scheme of Church government repudiates catholicity, and brings back the local and narrow polity of Judaism. She replaces Palestine with Italy, Jerusalem with Rome, the Temple with the Vatican, and the High Priest with Pontifex Maximus, the Pope. As the ancient Jew was obliged, like Daniel, when he prayed in Babylon with his windows open toward Jerusalem, to look to the Temple on Mount Zion for God's presence and favor, so the subject of Papal obedience, be he where he may on the earth's surface, must look to the Pope in the Vatican for his priesthood and his sacraments. The local episcopate in every land is simply the creation of the Bishop of Rome, his representative and his agent; all churches the wide world over in communion with the Pope are simply *colonies of Rome,* absolutely dependent upon her for officers and laws and absolution and benediction. Under her government the earth is unified from an earthly centre, not a heavenly, and the whole world is ruled by a worldly sovereign, seated on a local throne. The organization is grand, comprehensive, and unique, but it is not the system arranged by Christ, and worked out by the Apostles and their associates under the direction of the Holy Ghost. It is inconsistent with Scripture, irreconcilable with history, and repugnant to catholicity.

The inquiry is spontaneous, and, we are willing to allow, may be justly pressed upon our attention and claim from us a reply. How do you account for the phenomenon, if its origin be not of God? Can you on any other theory explain the rise and growth of the Papal power, if you refuse to admit that it is Divine? We answer that we can to our own satisfaction trace its development to human causes, which adequately and completely solve the difficulty. We proceed at once to catalogue and discuss the elements which enter into the complex problem, premising the remark that, even supposing we were not able to account for the Papal power, as it confronts us to-day, as a mere human growth, the alternative would not be that it must needs then be Divine; it is possible, nay, highly probable, that we are not properly qualified for the task, and, in the first place, have not brought forth all the causes which have been active in history in producing this result, and, in the second place, we have not done justice to those which we have adduced.

First, then, and before all other causes which have contributed to produce the Papal Power, is the city where it has its home. Rome, the ancient city, the seat of universal empire, the mistress of the nations, was the suggestion and the inspiration of what we call Romanism. This wonderful city embodied and kept before the minds of men ideas which are in their essence eternal truths, and which are imposing, grand, and fascinating—ideas which, when once grasped, cannot be dismissed; these ideas are unity through universal empire, centralization, organization, and obedience, passing in gradation from the lowest to the highest, from the many to the few, and from the few to the one, the universal monarch, the Cæsar on his throne. See how these ideas kept their place in the sphere of politics during the Middle Ages; note how they linger still. Even the names are not forgotten, and Roman Empire and Kaisar are still on men's lips as living words of the present. The Church founded in Rome by the Apostles inherited these ideas. They came perforce, without her will or choice, into her possession. They became a suggestion, they were even more, they were cherished as an inspiration. As soon as the Church of Rome emerged from the Catacombs, and was released from the blows of persecution, she found herself the first, the foremost Church of all her fellows. Thus she received from her city, whose growth and grandeur we have already sketched, the impulse which set her well on her way toward claiming more and more, as time went on, what came into her hands as men say "accidentally, in the natural course of events." A colossal city or diocese makes a colossal bishop. In one sense, as touching their office, all bishops are equal; in another sense, as regards the material interests which they represent, bishops are unequal, and often very unequal. For instance, when you look at our office, the Bishop of New York and the Bishop who addresses you are on a level, the one can do as much and no more than the other, but there the equality ceases. The Bishop of New York has behind him the mightiest city in wealth and population in the Western world; he represents in a sense these stupendous factors of material and worldly prowess, and his influence is correspondingly great. The other bishop represents poverty, weakness, sporadic elements of life few and far between, scattered over an immense territory. What comparison then is there between them on any plane where material interests are involved? And, further than this, when you pass into any field of discussion, however far removed from the sphere of what is distinctly secular, what chance has the little bishop against the great? Men do not care to oppose the mighty, those who can snub, and thwart, and possibly crush. They pay court to the great, and defer to them and wait upon their smile, and eagerly seek to anticipate their wish. And, then, so weak and naughty is the human heart, so easily is it puffed up with pride, that the occupants of these great sees often and quickly educate themselves to believe that they are really and intrinsically better than their fellows, that God has put a difference between them and others. Such are the tendencies inherent in the facts. A colossal city makes a colossal bishop, and this principle reached its maximum embodiment in Rome. *The greatest City of the World made the greatest Bishop of the World.* Even when the Empire was heathen the City lifted the Bishop so high that he drew to himself the unwelcome attention of the secular power, and in succession, in consequence, as in no other see, the early Bishops of Rome were martyrs. When the Empire became Christian, Rome's place was recognized as first, and the principle on which that primacy rested was clearly and accurately defined when the Second General Council, acting on this principle, assigned to the new seat of empire, Constantinople, the second place; it was the principle, namely, of *honor, based upon material greatness.* That this principle of graduation was speedily obscured and lost sight of is true, but still it maintained its hold upon the legislation of the Church through what we may call the conciliar period, and finds expression in the closing enactments of Chalcedon. Indeed, the principle of *the primacy*, as distinguished from *the supremacy* growing out of Petrine claims, was the heart and soul of Gallicanism in contrast to Ultramontanism, and was crushed out even in the Roman communion not twenty years ago. The mighty prestige of the City of Rome, her material greatness, as by far in advance of all others the first in the world, set her bishop equally far ahead of all competitors, and then, added to this material base from which his superiority rose, there floated round him hazy clouds of tradition which coupled his secular primacy of place with the spiritual claims of association with the Prince of the Apostles, as being the successor of S. Peter. And thus fact and fancy helped to inspire Rome almost from the outset with the ideas of primacy, grounded on more than the accident of place, and domination, resting on stronger claims than those afforded by secular power.

In the second place, Rome was an *apostolic see*, and this honor gave her an immense advantage in weight and influence in the mind of the primitive and early Church. An apostolic see is one that was founded by an Apostle, and its value consisted in the fact that its history went back to the Twelve, to those who had been with our Lord. It will at once be seen that in any discussion touching doctrine it was a matter of great importance to have access to a stream which flowed from an apostolic fountain, whose waters came down from S. Peter, or S. John, or S. Paul, or S. James. The succession of bishops was adduced in ancient times, not for the purpose of establishing the continuity of office, about that there was no question in those days, but with a view to establish the continuity of doctrine, to show that the alleged truth had been held without interruption, back and back by each bishop as he entered upon his office, for he then made a solemn profession of his faith, until the origin of the see was reached. The value of this witness would be in proportion to its antiquity, to the nearness of its approach to apostolic times, and it would rise to the maximum of weight, the utmost limit of influence, when it was *an apostolic see*, a bishopric founded by an Apostle in person. Rome's pre-eminence in this particular consisted not alone in the fact that it was an apostolic see, but still further in the additional fact that it enjoyed *a monopoly* of this distinction in the West. There were *many* apostolical sees in the East—Jerusalem, Antioch, Cæsarea, Ephesus, for example; there was *only one* of undoubted apostolical origin in the West, *and that was Rome.* This proud pre-eminence helped to fill men's minds with awe and reverence. It added immensely to her authority, and reacted upon her to impress her with exalted ideas of her own majesty and greatness.

Closely associated with the fact that Rome was an apostolic see, *the apostolic see of the West*, was the additional fact that, in the controversies which for three centuries raged around the Person and the

Natures of our Lord, and the Divinity and Person of the Holy Spirit, Rome was uniformly and steadily in the right until we reach the age of Honorius and the question of the one or two wills in the incarnate Christ. Meanwhile, the other patriarchates fell into heresy, first one, and then another, then two at once, then three, and then all four together; but Rome maintained her integrity, and as time went on her moral influence grew with more than arithmetical progression. To be right once when others go wrong may be an accident, and this may be the explanation a second time; but it will be hard to persuade men that it is still an accident when a third, and fourth, and fifth time the right is still maintained by the same party, while all the others have been once or twice or thrice in error. Such was Rome's position among the patriarchates during the fourth, and fifth, and sixth, and part of the seventh centuries; she was uniformly right, they were seldom right—often wrong. Mankind learned to rely upon her, and in the event felt sure that they would not be disappointed in their confidence. The apostolic see of the West strengthened the claim of her august antiquity by repeatedly uttering her voice, and uniformly on the side of right and truth, for hundreds of years.

During these centuries, while Rome's power and prestige were steadily growing in the West the Northern barbarians were descending as waves of the sea upon Southern Europe, and sweeping all before them save what they chose to spare. In succession came the Goth, and the Vandal, and the Hun, and spread over the fair territories of ancient civilization like devouring beasts of prey. The only power which challenged and awakened their respect and awe was Christianity, all else they cast down and destroyed; the Church remained, and ultimately subdued her conquerors, and made their mightiest monarchs attend as lacqueys upon her Patriarchs, and hold their stirrups while they mounted their steeds, and walked beside them to advertise their submission to the spiritual power, to which they deemed it an honor to do menial service. When the barbarian, the element which was destined to shape and form the life and character and religion and manners of mediæval Europe, came first in contact with Rome, she was well on her way toward those high pretensions and lofty claims with which we are familiar. The rude, rough warriors from the North had never known Rome before, they were not acquainted with her origin and early history. They accepted her as they found her, and received all that she taught them as undoubted truth, hence the new population of Southern Europe, when won over to Christianity, became unwittingly a mighty helper to push the see of Rome on and up in her progress toward supreme spiritual dominion over the nations of the earth.

Legislation naturally followed in the wake of successful usurpation. The general drift of canonical enactment during the decade of centuries from Chalcedon was to aggrandize Rome as the centre and mistress of the West. Appellate jurisdiction, for instance, limited and conditioned, as a concession to Pope Julius, by Sardica, in the middle of the fourth century, had become coercive jurisdiction without restraint in the days of Charlemagne. Everything lent itself to produce this result; it was, as we would say, the sensible and wise thing to do. Rome possessed the apparatus which best qualified her for hearing and adjudging causes. Over and above her ecclesiastical exaltation and spiritual prestige as an apostolic see and the first of the Patriarchates, she drew to herself and kept in her service the best and ripest learning of the times; hers were the archives and records of the past, stored up in greater profusion than elsewhere; hers was the authority to provide all that was requisite for the hearing of causes, and hers was the power to carry out her decrees and execute her sentences when issued and pronounced. Thus there came gradually into her hands, largely by the force of circumstances, and largely through her own grasping ambition, chains, forged by Provincial Councils and National Assemblies, which bound and fastened the West in ecclesiastical and legal subjection to Rome.

During this same period another fruitful cause was negatively operating to lift the Patriarchate of Rome high above all her competitors, and leave her in possession of the field as practically the head of

Christendom and the foremost Church of all the world, in the East as well as the West. A tree in the midst of a forest does not appear conspicuously great, but when the woodman has felled the grove with his axe and left but a single oak, it rises in lonely grandeur from the plain, and stands forth a giant in its proportions and its height. So it was with Rome; she left the period of the undisputed General Councils with *four sister Patriarchates*—Constantinople, Alexandria, Antioch, and Jerusalem. These were sufficiently on a level with her to contest her supremacy and check her growing pretensions. But within a century from the close of the Sixth General Council, *three* of these rivals of Rome were prostrate beneath the heel of the Moslem power, and the fourth was threatened. The followers of Mohammed overran and subdued Syria, Palestine, and Egypt, and drew near to the coasts of the Euxine and the Bosphorus, and with haughty effrontery lit their camp-fires and deployed their forces within sight of the Eastern capital. In the ninth century Alexandria and Antioch and Jerusalem ceased to exist as appreciable factors in the make up of Christendom, and Constantinople alone remained to occupy the ground as a rival of Rome. But she was at great and signal disadvantage as compared with her venerable competitor. She was not an apostolic see, she had no claims to prefer as a counter-charm to the name of Peter. She was crippled by the secular power, which continued by her side until Constantinople fell beneath the Turkish power in 1453. The Emperor and the State overshadowed her, and infused into her the poison of Erastianism; and meanwhile the Crescent went on increasing in conquests and nearness of approach to her, and at length, after centuries of imbecility, the city of Constantine became the capital of the Mohammedan Empire, and the Church of S. Chrysostom was converted into the Mosque of Santa Sophia. Then Rome was left really alone, she had been virtually so since the rise and success of the religion of the False Prophet. It had been Rome's advantage, on the other hand, that the seat of Empire in the West had at an early period been withdrawn from its old and immemorial home on the Seven Hills, and transferred to Ravenna, and then to Aix-la-Chapelle, and then fell apart into several divisions, no more to reappear in reality, or even in name, in Italy. Thus the Papacy was left without a companion to carry on and illustrate the traditions of the venerable past, secular as well as sacred. She improved her opportunities grandly, and grew apace in assertion and pretension and claim, with no voice in all the world that had the power to make itself heard to say her, nay.

Forgery and deception were employed to give the apparent support of antiquity to the extravagant claims of the Roman See in the ninth and tenth centuries. Alleged decretals of early Popes were imposed upon the credulity of an uncritical age as genuine documents, and doubtless honestly accepted and asserted as true even by Roman Bishops themselves. So far as the effect was concerned it is of no consequence whether the Popes were originally parties to the fraud or not. We are disposed, however, to acquit them of this immorality, and are of the opinion that they were originally devised and put in circulation in the interests of diocesan bishops as a protection against the tyranny of their metropolitans. Rome, however, was only too eager to use the weapon placed at her disposal, and long after she knew that they were spurious she appealed to them in quarters where she could safely do so to justify her claims. With the false decretals we must associate such forgeries as the Donation of Constantine, and wholesale corruptions of the early Fathers, as a fruitful cause for aggrandizing the Papacy and persuading mankind to accept it as a Divine system rooted in the earliest Christian antiquity.

The development of the Papal power was in accordance with the structure of society and the great institution of the Middle Ages, the feudal system. Then the spirit of the age was *centripetal*, as, since the Reformation, it has been *centrifugal*. Then the forces of secular and religious life sought the centre, as now they fly away from restraint and control. Familiarity with subordination, reaching from the serf to the monarch and uniting many and diverse elements under one supreme head in the State, reconciled, if it did not force men to desire a similar perfection of organization in the Church. The spirit of the age is a potent influence, and penetrates and is felt everywhere. The spirit of centralization was dominant in the olden time, as the net product of the civil and military structure and genius of pagan Rome, and of their offspring the feudal system of the Middle Ages. Everything tended that way and drifted in that direction, as we have seen the operation of opposite forces driving mankind asunder and producing an individualism so intense, that even those who have professed and called themselves Christians have held and taught that the zenith of human progress would be reached when every man was left free to do what was right in his own eyes. We must count, then, the spirit of the age as an important contributor to the growth and development of the Papal power.

But over and above all the causes which we have noted as combining to account, on human grounds, for the marvellous phenomenon of Papal claims as displayed before our eyes in the Vatican, we must remember that good men and true all over the West deliberately did their utmost, by act and word and example and influence, during the Middle Ages to help on the development of the power of the Bishop of Rome. I compliment my hearers and readers when I say that I think so well of them that I am persuaded that, had they been living then, they would have done the same, as seeking to confer the greatest benefit in their power upon society. We are not all gifted with a foresight which enables us to look very far into the future, most of us can see only a little way, and hence we act, the majority of us, in reference to immediate results, or results not far removed from eye and operating cause.

It is astonishing how little is known, even in these days, when knowledge is universal almost, and claimed by its votaries to be comprehensive and profound, how little is known of the Middle Ages. Men affect to contemn them; they call them "dark," and rightly in a sense, for indeed they are usually very dark to those who are loudest in declaiming against them, as we have said. In order to do scant justice to this large tract of human history, which borders on our modern age and connects us with classical antiquity and the epoch of our Blessed Lord and His Apostles, let me ask you to look out upon Western Europe as it presented itself to the eye at the beginning of the sixth century. We look upon a barren waste, nay worse, we gaze upon the ruins of a world. The civilization which Pericles and Cicero knew is crushed beneath the violence and rapine of rude barbarians. Everything that is fair and beautiful seems sinking fast out of sight, and the future holds out no hope. We close our eyes in despair, and feel that all things must be overwhelmed in one universal cataclysm. We open them again, and Europe in the sixteenth century is spread beneath our gaze. The desert has become a cultivated and fruitful expanse, occupied by the nations which are now the dominant races of the earth. Christianity has its cathedrals, and churches, and hospitals, and asylums, and shelters for monks and nuns. Learning has its universities, and colleges, and schools, and libraries; trade and commerce have their guilds and associations; the useful industries have pushed themselves to the front, and made for themselves a place and a name to be known and respected; cities fair and opulent dot the map from Ireland to the Indies; finance has its centres, and is arranging and regulating its domain in preparation for the bank, and the bourse, and the exchange; in a word, as we look out and around, we feel ourselves to be at home, we recognize our ancestors and their institutions public and private, and the interval though great is still within grasp between themselves and us.

When was this great change accomplished? Why, during the very period which many at the present day seek to discount under the flippant descriptive epithet, "*the Dark Ages.*" Who were the workers who wrestled with the stubborn wilderness, and the more stubborn natures of brutish men, and brought out of desolation fertility, out of barbarism civilization, out of anarchy civil institutions and settled government, out of chaos order and security to life and limb and property? The very men whom the wiseacres of the nineteenth century, with their heads high in the air, as they strut and swagger with their little stock of superficial information picked up from newspapers and reviews and encyclopædias, affect to disparage as poor benighted monks, ignorant ecclesiastics, and mediæval drones. It would be an interesting spectacle to see such persons compelled to take their places in the witness-box and sustain an examination upon the period which they are not slow to proclaim that they pity and despise, and which, with a splendid irony of which they are entirely unconscious, they denominate "*dark.*" It would soon be painfully apparent that their description was correct, but in a sense they did not mean. Alas! the darkness is abysmal, but it is not the darkness of the ages, but the profound ignorance of our friends and neighbors who, parrot-like, repeat the current talk of the day, and praise or condemn as fashion and the popular voice bid them speak.

This wonderful era, the Middle Ages, was, as is necessarily implied in the description which we have given, a formative period; it witnessed a transition from wild confusion to order, regulated and settled by law in the State and in society. Among the instrumentalities which good men and true, during the first half of this interval, or possibly two-thirds, looked to and trusted as most effectual to repress violence and subserve the best interests of mankind, *was the Papal Power.* We have ventured to suggest that had we lived between the era, say of the fall of the Western Empire in A.D. 476, and the close of the thirteenth century, we would have acted zealously with those who sought to aggrandize the power and the influence of the Bishop of Rome. We admit that it was for those who lived at the time, and would have been for us, had we been their contemporaries, a huge mistake to adopt this course, but that was not the question; the issue for us to have met was, "What is best for mankind, as far as ordinary human wisdom can foresee?" and the answer would have been, a great central power, based upon religion and morals, commanding the reverence of society, brave enough to speak out for right and justice and truth, and strong enough to cause its voice to be obeyed. Such a power offered itself and pressed itself upon the acceptance of the world for the cure of its evils and the supply of its social and moral needs in the rapidly-growing influence of what was claimed to be S. Peter's Chair. We are not ignoring the immoralities which often disgraced the lives of the Popes, and the corruptions which were creeping into the system. We do not forget the pornography and the dicta of Gregory VII. and the schema of Innocent III., but at a distance, when there were few channels of communication, scandals, even in the lives of eminent persons, were not soon known, and even when discovered, were not soon or readily published far and wide, and perversions in doctrine and declensions in discipline and practice did not challenge immediate attention and rebuke in an uncritical age.

The Papal Power at a distance from Rome inspired awe and continued to command the highest reverence, in spite of the Johns, and Formosus, and Stephens, and Theodoras, and Marozias. It was perfectly natural that this should be so, because the drift of Papal influence, as exhibited in public in the great issues, aside from the aggrandizement of its own power, was generally on the side of equity, and justice, and righteousness. An illustration will best serve to make plain our meaning. Philip Augustus of France, a contemporary of King John of England, in defiance of God's law and the opinion of men, resolved to put away the wife of his youth, and enter into a guilty alliance with a disreputable woman. Who was there to say him nay? There was no public opinion, in the modern sense of the term; no public Press; no local tribunal to call him to account. Even the Church was powerless in her national councils to coerce him into a decent respect for good manners and morals; on the contrary, Philip compelled her in her local councils to sanction by her approval his vileness and wickedness.

Let him of the nineteenth century who hears or reads this statement be not overmuch shocked, as though we in our time never winked at vice in high places, nor connived at sin under the penalty of losing the favor of the great, or at the price of receiving the money or the patronage of the rich. Alas! considering all the circumstances of those who live and act, one age has not so much the advantage of another. Be that as it may, however, there seemed to be at the time of which we are speaking no power on earth to stay the French King in his career of foul wrong to his injured wife and Queen, until the case came by appeal of Ingelburga to Innocent III. He quickly decided the issue in favor of innocence and right, and bade the monarch to put away his mistress and reinstate his wife. Philip demurred, and sought by every means at his command to cajole the Pope into acquiescence in his crime, but the Bishop of Rome sternly refused to listen to his flatteries or receive his bribes. He brought to bear upon him excommunication and interdict, and in six months' time Agnes was an outcast, and Ingelburga was in her lawful place. Think of the moral effect of such a spectacle presented and kept before the eyes of Europe.

Is it any wonder that good men would hail the Papacy in such an age, when there seemed to be no other power on earth strong enough to redress the terrible wrongs which were wrought by kings, and princes, and barons, and to cure the evils which were preying upon society? It is perfectly true that these good men were unwittingly helping to introduce and develop what would ultimately prove a worse evil than those which they sought to repress and expel; but they could not see into the distant future any more than we can. We have known a tender-hearted physician ply his patient, who was writhing with agony under the scourge of a painful disease, with nightly doses of morphine. The narcotic gave immediate and grateful relief, and at length the sick man became well; but he arose from his couch with a worse and more terrible disorder than that of which he had been cured; the insidious drug had introduced a craving for stimulants, and the present relief from excruciating distress was replaced by a permanent mania for drink. Thus was it with those who welcomed the autocracy and supremacy of the See of Rome, in the eleventh and following centuries, as a panacea for the ills of society and of the state and of the Church; they little dreamed that they were aiding to bind Europe in chains, which would become so galling in two centuries or more that the nations, goaded to frenzy by exactions and repression and tyranny, would rise in wild revolt and burst them asunder. Yet so it was, and the great convulsion of the sixteenth century was the outcome of centralization pushed to the extreme, without limits or restraints from beneath, and with scarcely any acknowledgment of accountability to any power which reigned above. Looking over that remote past, and taking into account the conditions of society, the presence of evils which have long since disappeared, and the absence of restraints which are the creation of modern times, and sinking ourselves to the level of ordinary mortals, and allowing that we are not endowed with the gift of forecasting the future beyond the powers of prescience possessed by our ancestors, we shall be prepared to admit that good men and wise men were excusable, if not justified, in throwing their influence on the side of the Pope. At all events they did so, and continued to do so until the reforming councils of the fifteenth century were, after repeated efforts, shown to be powerless " to reform the Church in its head and members," the object for which they were convened; and it was seen that the Western Patriarchate was beyond control from within, and was now undoing, and more than undoing, all the good that it had once and for ages done, by its corruption in faith and morals, its usurpations and rapacity, and its intolerable claims. Then true men and good men largely began to draw off from giving it their support with a view to aggrandize its power, and sought to put canonical restraints upon it, or else they took up a position of open revolt.

Thus the elements which might have saved it from the terrible catastrophe which has overtaken it in the Vatican decrees of 1870 were so reduced in strength, after the upheaval and disruption of the sixteenth century, that they were unequal to the effort of making head against the centripetal forces which had been for centuries driving Rome on to the awful plunge which she made when she disowned, by formal decree and as a matter of faith, the corporate government, as constituted and established by Christ, and substituted in its place another of her own invention—an absolute monarchy vested in a single potentate, not only free from limitation and irresponsible to man, but alleged to be and acknowledged to be infallible. This is the phenomenon which now confronts us, and we claim that we have abundantly accounted for its existence by the causes which we have adduced. God's word and God's will can have nothing whatever to do with a system which would make Him, if it were of Divine origin, flatly contradict Himself. It has been built up by human instrumentalities, and the result is an awful impiety, as we firmly believe, because it has attempted to invade Christ's sovereignty, and amend and repeal His laws. Place the Papacy as organized by the Schema of Pius IX., as it exists now, leaving out of view all the accidents of time and place, all the accessories which are not essential, face to face with the form of government established by our risen Lord, and vested by Him, as His last act while He remained on earth, in His eleven Apostles; face to face with the form of government administered by those same Apostles, as recorded by the Blessed Spirit in the inspired word of God; and it will at once be apparent that they are irreconcilable. The one is not derived from the other, as a flower from the bud or fruit from the blossom. The latter could only take the place of the former by *revolution*. There must have been the acts of breaking down and destroying, and then of substitution. And this exactly describes the process.

In this way modern Romanism occupies the seat of the ancient Catholic Patriarchate of the West. Practically, this has been the case for a long time, but as a matter of law and of faith it has only been so since 1870. Up to that date Gallicanism—which regarded the Pope simply as the *administrative head of Christendom*—was possible. Since that date and henceforth, until the Vatican decrees are repealed, such a view in the Roman Communion is heresy, and subjects him who maintains it to the pains and penalties of excommunication. We see, then, how very modern modern Romanism is. What place can such a system have in any movement toward Christian unity? "*Just none at all*" is the terse and definite answer which Rome herself compels us to make. In her present attitude, as defined by herself, she has isolated herself from the rest of Christendom. She has put up the bars against all approach from without, and has proclaimed and published the declaration that only on her own terms will she hold communion with her sister Patriarchates, or with any who profess and call themselves Christians, and those terms all outside of the obedience of the Pope believe to be disloyalty to Christ and treason against His Church. Surely it is useless, and worse than hopeless, to consider Rome in any efforts toward healing the present unhappy divisions of Christendom. She is the most unhistoric of sects. Her origin, as exhibiting a system which she enjoins as of faith, goes back no further than 1870. A Christianity which is not historic, which cannot trace its organic life in polity, faith, sacraments, and liturgy back to the Apostles, and through them find shelter under Christ's charter and constitution, cannot make good its claim to be Christ's Church, as He established it on the Mount of Ascension, and His Apostles, acting under His explicit directions, and guided and sustained by the Holy Ghost, organized it on the day of Pentecost, and administered it in all parts of the world whithersoever they went as the pioneer missionaries of the Gospel. What God has in store for Rome we know not; but as she stands before us to-day we can see no prospect of reaching her on any terms, save her own, which would be, as we account it, an absolute and complete surrender of Catholicity, and treason against Christ, and disloyalty to His Church. We are hopeless, so far as human foresight can reach, of Rome's reforming herself, and receding from her present position of isolation from the rest of Christendom, and returning to her place as a Patriarchate among Patriarchates.

The only ground for hope which we can discover for the Papacy is bound up in the success of the efforts for the accomplishment of Christian unity. If that blessed result is ever gained, then perchance the entirety of Christianity without Rome can constrain her to see her unchristian attitude and state, and to desire and seek to resume her place once more as a branch of Christ's Church. We admit that the prospect is very far from being encouraging; still, we may ask, is it any more gloomy than that of the conversion of the Jews? Our first duty is to labor for the unity of Christendom outside of Rome ; and in this field of noble endeavor it seems to me that we of the American Church have a very special vocation from God, made plain before our eyes by the providential position which we hold in relation to our fellow Christians. On the positive side we possess the deposit of Holy Orders, Faith, Sacraments, and a pure Liturgy ; on the negative we are, while being a historic Church reaching back without break or interruption to the Apostles, free from all the complications which embarrass older members of the Christian Commonwealth, who have had their feuds and quarrels, and retain their irritations and jealousies, which are the inheritance of the past. We are the young daughter of ancient parentage, planted on virgin soil, with no bitter recollections of our own to cherish ; and certainly, as yet, with years too few behind us to have enabled us to have left with others unpleasant memories of ourselves. Again, we are unembarrassed with any relations to the State. We are in the same condition in which the Early Church was before the days of Constantine. Locally, we are the connecting link between the old world on the East and the West. We reach from the Atlantic to the Pacific. We brought the historic Episcopate from Scotland in 1784, and from England in 1787 and 1790, and planted it in Connecticut, and New York, and Pennsylvania, and Virginia, and within a century we have carried it to California, and Oregon, and Washington Territory. We have Europe behind us, and Asia before us, and we are between, and the Patriarchates of the East are coming to our shores and making their homes among us. Surely Providence seems to be calling us by many unmistakable signs to become the great instrument in God's hands of effecting the unity of Christendom. Let us seek to enlighten ignorance and disarm prejudice; let us be true to the sacred office which God has assigned us, to hold in trust for mankind the treasures of Holy Orders, the Catholic Faith, the Sacraments, and the Liturgy; let us, as our supreme duty and highest pleasure, steadfastly speak to all " the truth in love"; and then we may be granted in time, it may be far on in the future, still we may be granted the glorious honor and the celestial happiness of giving the highest and best meaning to our national motto "*E pluribus unum*," when the American Church shall become the peacemaker among the dissentient members of the family, and the accepted medium through which they will again unite in communion, and so the divisions of Christendom will be healed, and out of the many branches there will appear to be once more, as of yore, but one Church under Christ, the Supreme Head, on His throne in heaven—one out of many in Him, as He is one with the Father, they in Him and He in them.

A lecture, supplementary to this course, entitled, "THE PATRIARCHATE OF CONSTANTINOPLE AND THE CHURCH OF THE EAST," was delivered at Christ Church on the seventeenth of May, 1888, by the Reverend JACOB S. SHIPMAN, D.D., D.C.L.

This lecture will not be found in this volume for the reason that the manuscript was not received in time for publication.

It is hoped that this lecture, however, may be put before the public at some later date.

www.ingramcontent.com/pod-product-compliance
Lightning Source LLC
Chambersburg PA
CBHW070737160426
43192CB00009B/1477